Secrets

OF THE *Bible*

Timothy J. Dailey, Ph.D.

Consultant:
David M. Howard, Jr., Ph.D.

Publications International, Ltd.

Louis Weber, C.E.O.
Publications International, Ltd.
7373 North Cicero Avenue
Lincolnwood, Illinois 60646

Permission is never granted for commercial purposes.

Manufactured in U.S.A.

8 7 6 5 4 3 2 1

ISBN: 0-7853-3239-1

Author: Timothy J. Dailey earned his doctorate in theology from Marquette University and studied at Wheaton College and the Institute of Holy Land Studies, Jerusalem. He has taught theology, biblical history, and comparative religion in the United States and Israel including at the Biblical Resources Study Center, Jerusalem, and Jerusalem Center for Biblical studies.

Consultant: David M. Howard, Jr., is associate professor of Old Testament and Semitic Languages at Trinity Evangelical Divinity School and holds a Ph.D. in Near Eastern Studies from the University of Michigan. He is the author of *Fascinating Bible Facts* and his writing credits include contributions to *The International Standard Bible Encyclopedia, Anchor Bible Dictionary,* and *Peoples of the Old Testament World*. He is a member of the Society of Biblical Literature and the Institute for Biblical Research.

Editorial assistance: Loren D. Lineberry

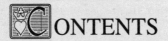ONTENTS

About the Bible

he earliest books of the Bible were written approximately 3,500 years ago; the last were written a little less than 2,000 years ago. Also, in what today would be considered an editorial nightmare, the 66 Books of the Bible were written by about 40 different authors.

The first part of the Bible, customarily called the Old Testament, is made up of 39 books translated from Hebrew and Aramaic, the ancient languages of the Jews. Most were dictated by their authors to professional scribes. Tradition holds that Ezra (whose story is told in the book bearing his name) compiled those 39 books, but there is no evidence to prove this.

An amazing discovery made in 1947 confirms that the scribes who made copies of the Hebrew Scriptures did an excellent job. In caves discovered near the Dead Sea, old jars were found containing ancient copies of 38 books of the Hebrew Scriptures (only Esther was not among the scrolls). These well-preserved copies had extraordinarily few differences from those that had been copied and recopied for millennia.

Notably, "Old Testament" is a misnomer. First, it implies that a "New Testament" follows, which, of course, did not happen for more than fifteen hundred years. Today, it is only called the Old Testament when referring to the first part of the Christian Bible. While there is some disagreement regarding what it should be called outside of that context, "Hebrew Scriptures" is generally accepted when referring to the Text used by the Jewish religion.

The New Testament was written over a span of about 50 years during the first century. Recording it was necessitated by the needs of the Early Church. As Jesus had done, his followers used the 39 books of the Hebrew Scriptures. Additionally, there were first-hand accounts of the life of Christ, which spread across the rapidly growing church. But as eyewitnesses began to die, it became necessary to write these accounts down, too. Thus we have the four gospels of Matthew, Mark, Luke, and John. Matthew and John were among Jesus' original 12 disciples. Mark and Luke were not. They traveled with St. Paul and wrote what they heard from the eyewitnesses.

These four books as well as letters written by Paul and other apostles, bolstered the Early Church. Then, during the third and fourth centuries, the New Testament was formally established. It contained the Gospels and the Letters (or Epistles), as well as the remaining books. It was very similar to the New Testament as we know it today.

Because the Bible is considered the Word of God for one of the world's largest religious groups, it is inherently mysterious. *Secrets of the Bible* elaborates on many of these mysteries, providing reasonable explanations for some. For others there are theories about what may be behind the secrets generated by the Holy Writ, plus what proof there is to support or disprove each hypothesis.

Whether you are familiar with the Scriptures or are simply intrigued by the "unknowns" that inundate the universe, the many mysteries contained in *Secrets of the Bible* are sure to pique your interest.

THE GARDEN OF EDEN
Can Paradise Be Found?

s the Garden of Eden merely a fanciful legend? If so, it is curious that the geographic description of it found in Genesis is more detailed and specific than that of most other biblical locations. This observation has aroused the interest of scholars and adventurers through the ages.

According to the Bible, the garden where the first humans dwelled was located "in Eden, in the east" (Genesis 2:8). A river flowed from the garden and divided into four head streams. Many scholars have thought that if they could establish the identity and location of these rivers the Garden of Eden could not be far beyond.

There is little question about two of the rivers mentioned in the text, the Tigris and Euphrates. Both exist today, in Iraq and Iran. A third river flowing from Eden was called the Gihon, which "flowed around the whole land of Cush" (Genesis 2:13).

The mention here of Cush has puzzled Bible scholars because it usually refers to a completely different geographical region—the area south of Egypt now known as Sudan. In Genesis, the area of Cush is associated with Nimrod, the founder of Babylon. This would put Cush in the region of the four rivers. One possible location is what is now a dry gully in Iran called Wadi Karun, which joins the Tigris and Euphrates rivers at the head of the Persian Gulf.

Scholars have long been curious about the last of the four rivers mentioned in Genesis, the Pishon. The text tells us more about the Pishon than any of the other rivers. We learn, for example, that "it is the one that flows around the whole land of Havilah, where there is gold; and the gold of that land is good; bdellium and onyx are there" (Genesis 2:11–12).

Havilah has been identified with the Arabian peninsula because the region—and particularly Yemen—was the historic source for highly prized fragrant resins such as frankincense and myrrh. The reference to high-purity gold has prompted scholars to look for evidence of ancient mines in the peninsula.

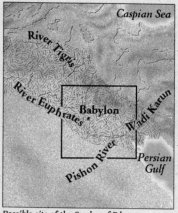

Possible site of the Garden of Eden.

Only one site in Arabia fits the description: the famous Mahd edh-Dhahab, or "Cradle of Gold." The mine is approximately 125 miles south of Medina near the Hijaz Mountains and is known to have been operating in ancient times.

Other intriguing evidence has recently become known regarding the location of the Pishon River mentioned in Genesis. For some time, scholars have suspected that a dry riverbed in Iraq called Wadi Batin might be associated with the biblical Pishon. Wadi Batin runs directly into the head of the Persian Gulf at the junction of the other three biblical rivers, and satellite photos have confirmed the presence of an underground river running below it. An analysis of the geographical features illuminated by the photos extends that underground river to the mountains of Hijaz.

Is this underground river the remnants of the Pishon River of Genesis? The fact that it leads to the gold of the Hijaz mountains and the aromatic spices of Yemen lends support to that thesis. And if the four rivers running out of Eden can be identified, perhaps the location of the primordial garden paradise will also one day be revealed. Unfortunately, if that day ever comes, deep-sea diving equipment may be required to view it. Some believe that the garden lies hidden underneath the headwaters of the Persian Gulf, not far from where the four rivers empty into it.

Who or What Are Cherubim and Seraphim?

According to the Bible, there are beings known as cherubim that are neither human nor divine.

The cherubim of the Bible are powerful, mysterious creatures, not to be confused with the chubby winged infants of medieval art. One of their functions seems to be that of guardians, and it is in this capacity that we find them first mentioned after the fall of man: "He drove out the man; and at the east of the Garden of Eden he placed the cherubim, and a sword flaming and turning to guard the way to the tree of life" (Genesis 3:24).

One might infer here that the cherubim are intended not only to guard but to conceal the location of the Garden of Eden from people. If so, it is tempting to speculate that this is one reason why the garden has been lost to history.

The next mention of cherubim is when these angelic creatures are represented in the Tabernacle that God commanded the Israelites build during their wanderings in the wilderness. Golden cherubim adorned the Ark of the Covenant, located in the Holy of Holies, the inner sanctuary of the Tabernacle. Cherubim were also depicted in the woven tapestry of the curtain in front of the Holy of Holies.

Raphael's representation of Ezekiel's cherubim.

The cherubim on the Ark are similar to beings depicted elsewhere in the ancient Near East. Together they form a throne, with their backs serving as armrests and their wings forming a backrest. The idea of a cherub throne is indicated in other biblical texts as well.

In the vision of Ezekiel, the description of cherubim closely resembles beings called seraphim. The word literally means "the burning ones." Such creatures are known from ancient Egypt, where they were depicted as winged serpents that decorated the thrones of pharaohs.

In the Book of Isaiah, seraphim are depicted as marvelous creatures that utter perpetual praise to God: "In the year that King

Uzziah died, I saw the Lord sitting on a throne, high and lofty; and the hem of his robe filled the temple. Seraphs were in attendance above him; each had six wings: with two they covered their faces, and with two they covered their feet, and with two they flew. And one called to another and said: 'Holy, holy, holy is the Lord of hosts; the whole earth is full of his glory'" (Isaiah 6:1–3).

What are we to make of such creatures? Scholars have sought in vain to fully explain them. The reason may be that cherubim and seraphim are by their very nature beyond human comprehension.

The Scarlet Thread

 he fourth chapter of Genesis tells of the birth of Adam and Eve's first two offspring, Cain and Abel. In a few short verses a story of a savage jealousy unfolds that ends with one brother killing the other.

The first sign of trouble came when we read that "Abel was a keeper of sheep, and Cain a tiller of the ground" (Genesis 4:2). One day the brothers brought offerings to the Lord. Abel brought "the firstlings of his flocks, their fat portions," (Genesis 4:4) while Cain brought "the fruit of the ground" (Genesis 4:3). The offerings did not meet with equal acceptance. The Lord "had regard for Abel and his offering" (Genesis 4:4) but not so with that of Cain.

Why was Abel's animal offering pleasing to the Lord while Cain's offering from his fields was not? Other biblical references to this story shed little light on the reason. They only confirm that Cain "was from the evil one" and murdered his brother because "his own deeds were evil and his brother's righteous" (1 John 3:12).

In trying to explain this story, some have theorized that it refers to the age-old tensions between farmers and nomadic shepherds, with the former seeking to protect their crops from the latter's flocks. But with the earth as yet unpopulated and there being more than sufficient space for both flocks and fields, it is unlikely that such tensions would have arisen. Also, this theory does not explain the superiority of one offering over the other.

Other scholars see a thread in this story that begins in the Garden of Eden and runs throughout the Bible—that of the necessity of blood sacrifice. The first inklings of this theme occur when Adam and Eve are cast out of the Garden of Eden for their disobedience. To cover their nakedness, Adam and Eve "sewed fig leaves together and made loincloths for themselves" (Genesis 3:7). However, this was apparently not sufficient, for we read that the Lord God "made garments of skins for the man and his wife, and clothed them" (Genesis 3:21).

What was wrong with the clothes that Adam and Eve fashioned for themselves? It is suggested that the killing of animals to provide covering for Adam and Eve is the first indication of what is later stated in the book of Hebrews: "without the shedding of blood there is no forgiveness of sins" (Hebrews 9:22).

The theme of blood sacrifice is developed in the Book of Leviticus, which details various types of animal offerings. The massive Altar of Sacrifice, upon which animals were slaughtered for the sins of the people, would later be a prominent feature of the Jewish Temple.

But such sacrifices were never quite sufficient. According to the Book of Hebrews, blood atonement for sin culminates in the sacrificial death of Jesus Christ on the cross: "How much more will the blood of Christ, who through the eternal Spirit offered himself without blemish to God, purify our conscience from dead works to worship the living God!" (Hebrews 9:14). Thus, the "unblemished" sacrifice of the Son of God is foreseen in Abel's sacrificing the "firstborn of his flock" to the Lord.

Cain was filled with jealousy toward his brother when his own offering was rejected despite the counsel of the Lord: "If you do well, will you not be accepted? And if you do not do well, sin is crouching at the door; its desire is for you, but you must master it" (Genesis 4:7).

Cain's response is made clear in the next verse. He invites his brother out into the fields and murders him. As punishment, Cain was no longer able to till the ground and was condemned to be a "wanderer on the earth" (Genesis 4:12).

Where Did Cain Find His Wife?

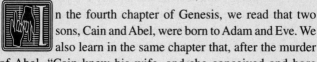 n the fourth chapter of Genesis, we read that two sons, Cain and Abel, were born to Adam and Eve. We also learn in the same chapter that, after the murder of Abel, "Cain knew his wife, and she conceived and bore Enoch" (Genesis 4:17).

Presumably, Cain married one of his sisters. Close inter-marriage was not forbidden then. Indeed, it could hardly have been avoided in the early days of the human race. It was not until the time of Moses that the sanction against brother-sister mar-riages was spelled out.

Still, the question of where Cain met his wife is not quite solved. It is not until after the birth of his brother, Seth, that we hear mention of daughters: "The days of Adam after he became the father of Seth were eight hundred years; and he had other sons and daughters" (Genesis 5:4).

Is this text saying that daughters were only born *later* to Adam and Eve? And if so, we return to our original question of where Cain found his wife. The likely answer lies in the nature of ancient patriarchal society, which very often excluded women from genealogical lists, since men were viewed as the origina-tors of the family line. It is not surprising, then, that there would be no daughters of Adam and Eve mentioned in the text that speaks of Cain getting married. In fact, the names of the daugh-ters of Adam and Eve aren't mentioned anywhere in the bibli-cal text.

It is also evident that the biblical text is compressing huge amounts of time. Adam is said to have lived to be 930 years old. Since, according to the text, he was already 130 years old when Seth was born, he could have had many daughters by that time.

Much fascinating history must have gone unrecorded, at least in the biblical text. Although the record is silent regarding the identity of Cain's wife, she clearly has her place in the early history of the human race.

THE FLOOD
The Great Flood: Fact or Fiction?

he Bible tells us that, a mere ten generations after the creation of Adam and Eve, the wickedness of their descendants was such that "the Lord was sorry that he had made humankind on the earth, and it grieved him to his heart" (Genesis 6:6). Summoning the rain, he decided to destroy humankind with a massive flood so that he could start all over again.

The Lord found an exception in righteous Noah, deciding to spare him and his family, along with the animals and other living creatures. The ark Noah was instructed to build was actually a huge wooden barge. With a length of 450 feet, a width of 75 feet, and three interior decks reaching a height of 45 feet, it would have been the largest seagoing vessel known before the 20th century. Interestingly, its dimensions are remarkably similar to that of modern ships.

Scholars are divided as to the extent of the biblical flood, many holding that it may have been a local event limited to the Mesopotamian floodplain. The Bible, however, is unequivocal in stating that "all the high mountains under the whole heaven were covered" (Genesis 7:19).

Archaeologists have attempted to find evidence of such a flood in Mesopotamia. Their efforts have thus far proved inconclusive. In 1929, when English scientist Charles Leonard Woolley was excavating a Sumerian burial pit at Ur on the Euphrates River, his workers came upon a layer of silt more than eight feet thick. It contained relics of a different, more primitive culture. Woolley came to the conclusion that a great flood had occurred in the region sometime around the fourth millennium B.C. However, flood deposits discovered at other sites in Mesopotamia were dated to later historical periods, discrediting this theory.

Those who were not in the Ark.

In 1872, the publication of a cuneiform tablet from Nineveh on which was written an ancient Babylonian account of a very great flood rocked the scholarly world. The text is part of the classic Epic of Gilgamesh. The hero of the story is Utnapishtim of Shuruppak, who is warned that Enlil, the chief god of the Babylonian pantheon, would soon destroy humankind with a flood. Utnapishtim was instructed to build an ark for himself and his family and "the seeds of all living things."

Unlike the biblical account of Noah's flood, in which the rains and floods continued for 40 days and nights, the floods in the Epic of Gilgamesh lasted only six days and nights.

Utnapishtim and his ark also come to rest on a mountaintop. Like his biblical counterpart, Utnapishtim opens a window and releases a series of birds to find out if the surface of the earth has dried sufficiently. In yet another parallel, Utnapishtim's first act upon leaving the ark is to build an altar and offer a sacrifice. Since the discovery of the flood story in the Epic of Gilgamesh, at least two other Mesopotamian flood stories have become known, both containing the same central features.

Scholars have long pondered the relationship between the Mesopotamian flood stories and the biblical narrative. Some have suggested that each of these accounts refers to the same cataclysmic flood. If so, then we should expect to find flood stories in other ancient cultures in other parts of the world. And this is exactly what ethnologists have discovered. James Frazer, a well-known student of religions around the world, has collected many flood stories—from places as diverse as Greece, the South Pacific, and the Americas. Such evidence presents at least the possibility that, at some time in prehistory, a worldwide flood of cataclysmic proportions occurred, surviving today only as a dim memory in the cultural traditions of peoples around the world.

Was Noah's Ark Big Enough?

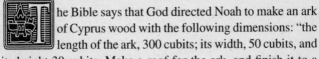 he Bible says that God directed Noah to make an ark of Cyprus wood with the following dimensions: "the length of the ark, 300 cubits; its width, 50 cubits, and its height 30 cubits. Make a roof for the ark, and finish it to a cubit above; and put the door of the ark in its side; make it with lower, second, and third decks" (Genesis 6:15–16).

Scholars have tried to ascertain the feasibility of such a vessel in light of our present-day knowledge of both shipbuilding and zoology. The Hebrew cubit was approximately 18 inches long, which meant that the ark would have been 450 feet long, 75 feet wide, and 45 feet high. This length-to-width ratio of six to one is considered ideal, and would have provided excellent stability for the ark on the open seas.

The boat in the Babylonian account of the Great Flood is described as a perfect cube with nine decks and extending 120 cubits on each side. Such a vessel would be top-heavy, causing it to spin, slowly and continuously, in the water.

The second part of the question is whether the ark would have been large enough to fit all the animals that would have needed to go inside. The floor space would have been more than 100,000 square feet, or more than in 20 basketball courts. With a volume of 1,518,000 cubic feet, it would have had a capacity equal to 569 modern railroad cars.

But how many of earth's animals would have had to be taken aboard the ark? Of the more than one million species of animals in the world, the vast majority can survive in water and would not have been brought aboard. These include 21,000 species of fish; 1,700 species of tunicates (marine chordates such as sea squirts); 107,000 species of mollusks (mussels, clams, oysters); 10,000 species of coelenterates (corals, sea anemones, jellyfish, and hydroids); 5,000 species of sponges; and 30,000 single-celled protozoans.

Aquatic mammals also need not have been included. These include whales, seals, and porpoises. Reptiles such as sea turtles and alligators would have been excluded as well. The more than 838,000 arthropods—including lobsters, shrimp, crabs, and barnacles—would have survived outside the ark, as would many species of worms and insects.

Some scholars estimate that perhaps no more than 35,000 individual animals would have needed to go into the ark. Others, pointing out that the biblical term "created kinds" is more general than the modern term "specie," believe that as few as 2,000 animals would have been aboard the ark. Also, a single ancestral pair would have represented dozens of present-day species (consider the "microevolution" of dogs and horses).

Assuming that the larger animals could be represented by young (and therefore smaller) specimens, it is reasonable to assume the average size of all the animals to be that of a sheep. Returning to the boxcar comparison, a typical double-deck car can hold 240 sheep. Three trains hauling 69 cars each would have sufficient space for 50,000 animals—and that would only take up about one-third of the capacity of the ark. That would leave 361 cars for all the food and baggage, plus Noah and his family.

The Search for Noah's Ark

ccording to the Bible, Noah's ark came to rest on "the mountains of Ararat" (Genesis 8:4). The biblical Ararat is known in ancient sources as the land of Urartu, located north of Mesopotamia around Lake Van. Today Turkey, Iran, and Armenia occupy the region. After the flood, the ark disappears from the pages of Scripture. Later biblical writers gave no indications that its location was known. Throughout history, however, there have been many reports of a large boat sighted in the mountains of the region. The earliest references, dating to the third century, B.C., suggest that the ark was still clearly visible on the mountain.

Early Christian tradition began designating a 17,000-foot peak in northern Turkey as Mt. Ararat. At least two monasteries shaped like boats were built on the peak during the Middle Ages, and pilgrims were attracted to the area. In the past century there have been aerial photographs taken of unusual structures on the mountain, reports of visits to the ark, and even the recovery of wooden timbers. The suggested location of the ark is above the snow line, and it has been theorized that only during exceptionally warm summers do the snow and ice recede sufficiently for the ark to be seen. Complicating visits to the site is the fact that Mt. Ararat has until recent years been in a sensitive border region between Turkey and the former Soviet Union.

Nevertheless, during the past two decades dozens of expeditions have explored Mt. Ararat in hopes of finding evidence of the ark's existence. Perhaps the most famous were those organized and led by former NASA astronaut James Irwin. Unfortunately, these efforts have not been successful.

One of the most electrifying developments in the search for the ark occurred in 1955, when a French explorer named Fernand brought down a five-foot-long wooden beam from just beneath the glacial cap of Ararat. Finally, it seemed, indisputable proof of the ark had been discovered. But excitement turned to bewilderment when radiocarbon dating determined the wood to be no more than 1,200 years old.

Yet how could that be? What about the eyewitness reports of explorers visiting and even entering an arklike structure? Calculating the period to which the wood was dated finds the probable answer to such questions. It was the same as that of the boat-shaped monasteries built on the mountain. The presence of more than one such monastery may also explain the conflicting reports about the ark's precise location on the mountain.

This does not mean that Mt. Ararat holds no secrets. It is possible that the exploration of other peaks in the Ararat range will be undertaken, as efforts continue to find evidence of what may have been the most calamitous event ever to occur on this planet.

What Was the Tower of Babel?

he barren desert sands of southern Mesopotamia are the backdrop for one of the most mysterious Bible stories, that of the Tower of Babel. Its construction is said to be the reason why so many different languages are spoken in the world today.

Noah's son Ham had four sons, one of whom was Cush. Nimrod was Cush's son. According to Genesis 10:10, he was a mighty hunter with a sizable kingdom that started at Babel, in the land of Shinar.

The text of Genesis 11 states that "the whole earth had one language and the same words. And as they migrated from the east, they came upon a plain in the land of Shinar and settled there" (Genesis 11:2).

It wasn't long before they imagined a grandiose scheme: "Come, let us build ourselves a city, and a tower with its top in the heavens, and let us make a name for ourselves; otherwise we shall be scattered abroad upon the face of the whole earth" (Genesis 11:4).

The description of the building materials they used lends some authenticity to the text, for "they said to one another,

'Come, let us make bricks and burn them thoroughly.' And they had brick for stone, and bitumen for mortar" (Genesis 11:3). Interestingly, in ancient Israel, where the text originated, the use of fired bricks was unknown. Buildings were

Brueghel's Tower of Babel.

constructed either of stone or sun-dried bricks. But the use of fired bricks is well documented throughout Mesopotamia. The use of tar instead of mortar to cement bricks is another detail confirmed by archaeology.

But what exactly was the Tower of Babel, and what was the offense of the people who built it? Archaeology has given us clues to solving this mystery. Scholars believe that the "tower" of Babel was actually a ziggurat, a pyramidlike structure that played an important role throughout Mesopotamian civilization. Nearly 30 ziggurats have been found—and nearly as many theories exist as to what purpose they served.

What we know from ancient texts is that ziggurats were typically dedicated to a city's patron god or goddess. Beyond this, scholars disagree as to their specific purpose. It was once thought that ziggurats were the tombs of kings or the gods, based upon the obvious similarity in shape to the early Egyptian step-pyramid tombs. But the step-pyramids have been shown to be more recent structures, having been built more than a millennium after ziggurats began to dot the map of early Mesopotamia.

Others believe that ziggurats were actually towering altars that protected against flood and plunder. But this can hardly explain the massive size and height of some structures. The ziggurat dedicated to the god Marduk, which stood in the center of the city of Babel, reached the height of a 30-story building.

A more plausible theory is that a ziggurat served as the dwelling place for the local god or goddess, the entrance door through which they passed to the earthly plane. This is reflected in some of their names. The ziggurat at Larsa was known as "The Temple That Links Heaven and Earth"; the one at Sippar was called "The Temple of the Stairway to Pure Heaven."

If the theory is correct, this suggests that the ziggurats served a profoundly religious purpose. They were an attempt to draw the gods down to earth. And here we have a clue as to what may have been so objectionable to God about the Tower of Babel. It represented an attempt to reduce the deity to the level of human beings. And it shows them turning from trusting in God, to trusting in themselves.

THE PATRIARCHS
Abraham in History

he age of the biblical patriarchs remains shrouded in mystery. Some scholars believe that Abraham, Isaac, Jacob, and Joseph existed only in the pious imaginations of later Hebrew writers. Others feel this judgment is unwarranted.

Those who believe that the patriarchs are rooted in history say it is unreasonable to expect sources beyond the Bible to confirm events in the lives of Abraham and his offspring. The fact that a tent-dweller such as Abraham figures prominently in the Bible does not mean he merits attention in ancient Near Eastern historical records.

However, archaeologists have uncovered what some believe is a reference to the Hebrew patriarch in a nonbiblical record. It comes from the reign of Pharaoh Sheshonq I, whom many scholars equate with the biblical Shishak.

In the Book of 1 Kings we read of a campaign against Palestine by Shishak: "In the fifth year of King Rehoboam, King

Shishak of Egypt came up against Jerusalem; he took away the treasures of the house of the Lord and the treasures of the king's house; he took everything. He also took away all the shields of gold that Solomon had made" (1 Kings 14:25–26).

The Book of Chronicles gives a fuller account of the extent of Shishak's campaign, stating that it involved 1,200 chariots, 60,000 horsemen, and countless troops. We

Abraham journeys to the Land of Canaan.

read that Shishak "took the fortified cities of Judah and came as far as Jerusalem" (2 Chronicles 12:4), where disaster was averted when Rehoboam handed over the temple treasures.

If Pharaoh Sheshonq is to be equated with the biblical Shishak—and scholars are not agreed on this—we have an interesting parallel in an inscription in the Temple of Amun in Karnak. Throughout Egyptian history, whenever pharaohs returned from a victorious military campaign, they would usually record their triumph for posterity. At Karnak, archaeologists have deciphered a stela, or standing stone, on which Pharaoh Sheshonq describes his triumphant campaign against Israel.

Most of the perhaps 150 names on the stela have eroded and are unreadable. Of those that remain, perhaps 70 names come from the Negev, a desert in southern Israel. One of those has been identified by Egyptologists as the equivalent of the Hebrew "Abram." The phrase where the name occurs reads: "The fort [or fortified town] of Abraham."

Is the "Abram" of Fort Abram the biblical patriarch? Possibly. After all, the biblical Abraham lived in the Negev where this "Fort Abram" was located. Such an outpost may have been built in the time of David or Solomon as part of a line of fortifications against Egyptian intrusion. It would not be unusual for the fort to be named after some national hero or revered personage such as the patriarch.

Other scholars suggest that Fort Abram is actually Beersheba, a city founded by Abraham (Genesis 21:32–33). The reason behind this notion is that Beersheba is not mentioned elsewhere in Pharaoh Sheshonq's list. Since it was a prominent city in the Negev, its omission is unexplainable, unless, perhaps, it is the very same city called Fort Abram by the Egyptians.

If so, the connection with the biblical patriarch becomes probable, and it constitutes evidence that Abraham was a real person who lived in the memory, and in the place names, of the ancient Hebrews.

Mysterious Melchizedek

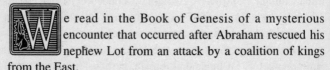 e read in the Book of Genesis of a mysterious encounter that occurred after Abraham rescued his nephew Lot from an attack by a coalition of kings from the East.

Upon his return he was met by a certain Melchizedek, king of Salem, who is called "a priest of the most High God." Melchizedek brought bread and wine and blessed Abraham: "Blessed be Abram by God Most High, maker of heaven and earth; and blessed be God Most High, who has delivered your enemies into your hand" (Genesis 14:19–20).

Curiously, we also read that Abraham gave him a tithe of one-tenth of all his goods. Who is this Melchizedek, king of Salem, who apparently commanded the reverence of Abraham?

The mystery of Melchizedek's identity deepens when the Book of Hebrews provides further information about him. We first learn that his name means "king of righteousness" as well as "king of peace" (Hebrews 7:2). And then comes an intriguing description of Melchizedek: "Without father, without mother, without genealogy, having neither beginning of days nor end of life, but resembling the Son of God, he remains a priest forever" (Hebrews 7:3).

The fact that he is spoken of as having no mother or father, and no beginning or end of days, has led some to wonder if he were some kind of divine personage. Most theologians, however, reject this possibility because it would ascribe to another being that which properly belongs only to God—that he is eternal. In the Judeo-Christian world view all creatures—even the angels— had a beginning.

So why does the Bible speak about Melchizedek in such terms? Again, many theologians believe that Melchizedek is used by the biblical writers as a "type" of Christ, someone who in some respects resembled the divine figure of the Messiah. And indeed, Melchizedek was an unusual figure who did seem to come "out of nowhere."

Salem (which would later become Jerusalem) was a Canaanite city that likely shared the polytheistic beliefs of the rest of the land, in contrast to Abraham and his clan, who believed in one god. That Abraham would have had nothing to do with the people or culture of such a "pagan" city is indicated by the story of the sacrifice of Isaac.

The text states that Abraham, Isaac, and a servant journeyed to "a mountain of the land of Moriah" (Genesis 22:2) to perform a sacrifice. Many scholars believe that this Mount Moriah is none other than the Temple Mount in Jerusalem. The text states that Abraham took fire with them for the anticipated sacrifice. This would seem to have been unnecessary because the city of Salem was located within a stone's throw of Mount Moriah. It would have been much easier for Abraham to procure fire there, rather than carry it for three days—unless, that is, he had no dealings with the Salemites.

Melchizedek would have been a mysterious and unknown personage from a strange city who suddenly appears on the scene. The text of Hebrews should then read, "Without any known father, without mother, with no known genealogy..." (Hebrews 7:3).

Nothing is known about Melchizedek's origins, and so in this respect he is like the Messiah, who comes from God. To emphasize his divinity, Jesus is described in Hebrews as "according to the order of Melchizedek," rather than being of the order of the earthly Aaronic priesthood. For the same reason, Psalm 110 speaks of the coming Messiah as being forever a priest in the "order of Melchizedek" (Psalm 110:4).

Sodom and Gomorrah

n the Book of Genesis we read that Abraham looked up from the entrance to his tent "by the oaks of Mamre" (Genesis 18:1–2) at Hebron to see three strange men standing nearby. In keeping with Middle Eastern custom, he invited the men inside his tent while a meal was being prepared for them.

We soon learn that two of the men were angels, while the third was the Lord himself. This is one of the rare occurrences in the Old Testament of what theologians call a theophany—a visible appearance of God.

It seems Abraham's guests had a dual purpose for their visit. The first was to announce that Sarah, then nearly 90 years old, would bear a son, a prediction that would be fulfilled with the birth of Isaac. Nothing is said about the second purpose until the men get up to leave. Then, looking down from the hill country of Judea to the Dead Sea, the Lord said: "How great is the outcry against Sodom and Gomorrah, and how very grave their sin! I must go down and see whether they have done altogether according to the outcry that has come to me" (Genesis 18:20–21).

What follows is a fascinating exchange in which Abraham tries to find out how few righteous people in Sodom would be required to save the city from destruction. First, he asks whether the Lord would spare Sodom if 50 righteous people were found there. Then he lowers the stakes to 40, to 30, and then to 20. Finally, he musters the courage to ask: "Oh, do not let the Lord be angry if I speak just once more. Suppose ten are found there?" The Lord answers: "For the sake of ten I will not destroy it" (Genesis 18:32).

Unfortunately, Sodom lacked even a bare quorum of ten. The story reads like an adventure, with moments of high drama in which the two angels are bold and fearless beings worlds apart from the innocent cherubs of religious art. They set off to visit Sodom and spend the night at Lot's home. The climax of the narrative comes when the men of the city come to Lot's home in the night demanding the men who came to him that night. "Bring them out to us, so that we may know them" (Genesis 19:5). Lot feebly offers his two daughters in exchange, which only enrages the men of the city, who order him to get out of their way.

As they surge forward to break down the door, the two angels move quickly. They pull Lot back into the house and shut the door. "And they struck with blindness the men who were at the door of the house, young and old, so that they were unable to find the door" (Genesis 19:11). There was no time to lose. The angels urged Lot and his family to leave the city at once. In a curious footnote to the story, we read that "Lot's wife, behind him, looked back, and she became a pillar of salt" (Genesis 19:26).

The Bible speaks of Sodom and Gomorrah as being among the five "cities of the Plain," which were likely located in the Valley of Siddim, adjoining the Dead Sea. Some scholars have suggested that Sodom and Gomorrah are located under the shallow southern end of the Dead Sea, where the water is less than ten feet deep in many places. However, aerial photographs of the area have shown no traces of an ancient settlement.

More recent investigation has focused on two sites directly bordering the Dead Sea to the east and south. The modern

Lot's wife turned into a pillar of salt.

name for these sites are Bab edh-Dhra, thought to be Sodom, and Numeira, thought to be Gomorrah. Excavations have revealed a layer of debris 3-feet-thick, with indications that both places were destroyed by an immense conflagration. A problem with this identification is the dating of these cities, which are several centuries before the usually accepted dates for Abraham. But further refinements of dating schemes may solve this puzzle.

But what could have caused such devastation? The description found in Genesis tells us that "The Lord rained on Sodom and Gomorrah sulfur and fire" (Genesis 19:24). The answer to the mystery may be found in the Dead Sea.

Geologists have long suspected the presence of oil underneath the Dead Sea because of the many reports throughout history of petroleum-based substances, such as bitumen, found in and around the body of water. Bitumen often contains a high percentage of sulfur, prompting some geologists to suggest that an earthquake in the area could have released huge quantities of subterranean gases and other flammable substances into the atmosphere. Once ignited, these substances could have created a conflagration of biblical proportions. Interestingly, geologists have discovered that both Bab edh-Dhra and Numeira are located on a fault line extending along the eastern side of the Dead Sea.

Did an earthquake cause the fiery devastation that consumed Sodom and Gomorrah? No one knows for sure, but at the close of the Bible story, we read that Abraham, looking down toward the two cities, "saw the smoke of the land going up like the smoke of a furnace" (Genesis 19:28). The description suggests a petroleum-based fire.

Israel's Ancient Enemy Unearthed

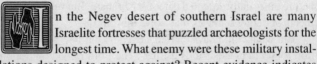n the Negev desert of southern Israel are many Israelite fortresses that puzzled archaeologists for the longest time. What enemy were these military installations designed to protect against? Recent evidence indicates that they were a frontline defense against Edom, Israel's ancient enemy.

The biblical story of Jacob and Esau is one of sibling rivalry that foreshadows the continuing strife in the Middle East. While the two brothers were still in the womb of Rebekah, the Lord said to her:

> "Two nations are in your womb,
> and two peoples born of you shall be divided;
> The one shall be stronger than the other,
> The elder shall serve the younger."
>
> —(Genesis 25:23)

Esau, the firstborn, was tricked by his brother Jacob into surrendering his birthright for a mess of pottage. Then, with Rebekah's connivance, Jacob deceived his dying father Isaac into giving him the blessing usually reserved for the firstborn son. Eventually, Esau took Canaanite wives and settled in the hill country of what today is southern Jordan—but which was then known as Edom.

Until recently, little was known of the nation that figured so prominently in Israel's early history. It was the Edomites who, despite assurances by the Israelites, refused to allow them to pass through their territory on their way to the Promised Land. The route that the Israelites desired to take was an ancient trade route known as the King's Highway. Edom would later pay for its hostility when it was attacked by King Saul and conquered by King David.

Archaeologists were surprised to discover evidence of Edomite cities in the Negev region of southern Israel. Some scholars think these cities date to the seventh century B.C., a time of political upheaval in Judea. The northern kingdom of Israel had fallen to the Assyrians, and the Babylonians were encroaching ever deeper into the southern kingdom of Judea.

The large number of ritual artifacts—including idols, incense altars, and cultic shrines—uncovered at the Edomite sites reflect the profusion of deities that the populace worshiped. Their polytheistic practices stand in marked contrast to the strict monotheism of the Israelite nation. The considerable religious and cultural differences between the two groups ensured that they would remain perpetually at odds, and it could possibly explain the reason for the line of Judean forts in the Negev.

Isaac mistakenly blesses Jacob as Rebekah stands watch.

Edom was destined to fade from history, but not before making its mark once more in the form of one of its most infamous descendants. By the fourth century B.C., the Edomites in the Negev were called by another name: Idumeans. The mother of Herod the Great was an Idumean who married a Judean. And so the two peoples were symbolically reunited in the turbulent person of Herod, a ruler legendary for his cruelty and insecurity.

Rachel's Premature Death

 ne of the most moving love stories in the Bible is that of Jacob and Rachel. Jacob saw the lovely Rachel bringing her sheep to water and was instantly smitten. He would work seven years for her father, Laban, for the right to marry her, followed by another seven years because of Laban's craftiness in tricking him.

The love they shared was made even more touching by the untimely death of Rachel during childbirth. From that time on, it is clear that Jacob favored Joseph and Benjamin, the two sons that Rachel bore him. When he is shown Joseph's bloody coat and believes him to be dead, Jacob is inconsolable. Later, he takes the unusual step of granting Joseph's two sons, Ephraim and Manasseh, equal inheritance rights to that of his other sons.

Jacob explains the reason he is doing this: "For when I came from Paddan, Rachel, alas, died in the land of Canaan on the way" (Genesis 48:7). Until the end of his life, Jacob was haunted by the death of his beloved Rachel. A startling reason has been suggested as to why Jacob was so troubled: He felt responsible.

To understand this, we must return to when Jacob and Rachel finally took their leave of Laban and set out for Canaan. Before they left, Rachel took her father's household idols, probably because of the good luck she thought they would bring. When he discovered that his idols were gone, Laban pursued Jacob and accused him of theft. Unaware that his wife had taken the idols, an indignant Jacob vowed that "anyone with whom you find your gods shall not live" (Genesis 31:32).

Oaths were considered binding in biblical times, and they often had unintended effects. By pronouncing judgment upon the guilty—even though he was ignorant of Rachel's action—he unwittingly condemned her to death. Rachel herself was unaware of Jacob's oath. While he was speaking with Laban, she was in her tent, guarding the idols by sitting on them.

After leaving Laban, Jacob was commanded by the Lord to go to Bethel and build an altar. Bethel was an important religious site for

Jacob with his father-in-law and two future wives.

the Hebrew patriarchs: It was here that Abraham "invoked the name of the Lord" (Genesis 12:8). Jacob had stopped at Bethel many years earlier on his flight from his brother Esau. During the night, he dreamed of a ladder going up to heaven. The Lord spoke to him, confirming the blessing originally given to Abraham.

In preparing for his arrival at the holy site of Bethel, Jacob instructed his family and servants: "Put away the foreign gods that are among you, and purify yourselves, and change your clothes; then come, let us go up to Bethel" (Genesis 35:2–3). It was likely he did not suspect Rachel had idols in her possession.

The text does not say that Rachel surrendered her idols at Jacob's command, it is reasonable to conclude that she did. The text states that the people with him "gave to Jacob all the foreign gods that they had" (Genesis 35:4). Rachel likely complied with the others, not having heard Jacob's fateful oath to Laban and being unaware of any consequences that would follow.

But the tragic consequences would follow all too soon. Doubtless with a heavy heart, Jacob left Bethel with his family. They do not get far, for we read that Rachel went into labor and died giving birth to her son Benjamin. And so Jacob buried her and went on his way, tormented by the fear that his hastily spoken oath may have been Rachel's death sentence.

WANDERING IN THE DESERT
The Parting of The Red Sea

ew events recorded in the Bible capture the imagination like the story of Moses parting the Red Sea. For contemporary Americans, actor Charlton Heston raising his staff over the waters in *The Ten Commandments,* the epic Cecil B. DeMille film, is a famous moment in film history.

Biblical scholars are divided as to the event. Did the Children of Israel cross a body of water that miraculously parted for them—or was it actually a marsh they crossed, which providentially happened to ensnare the chariots of the pursuing Egyptians?

Part of the mystery involves the identification of the Hebrew words *yam suf*, which are translated in some versions of the Bible as "Red Sea." Scholars have long known that the word "red" does not occur in *yam suf*. A better translation of the Hebrew words would be "Reed Sea"—a rendering that opens the possibility that the Israelites crossed a swampy area to the north of the Red Sea. Accordingly, many historical maps trace the route of the Exodus through the marshy Lake Timsah or Bitter Lake region.

This solution is not as simple as it seems. It cannot be denied that some biblical references to yam suf clearly refer to the Red Sea. Complicating the problem is the fact that the part-

The Israelites cross the Red Sea.

ing of the Red Sea is not mentioned in any contemporary Egyptian texts. Some have taken this as evidence that the event is mythological rather than historical. Yet the omission is not surprising.

The royal chronicles of ancient times were notorious for ignoring events that might cast the potentate in an unfavorable light. Not one reference can be found in Egyptian records, for example, that mentions the humiliating, century-long domination of Egypt by the Hyksos. Similarly, it would be hard to imagine any ancient potentate chronicling the loss of an entire army in pursuit of a mass exodus of unarmed slaves.

But how could the Israelites escape unscathed while Pharaoh's army perished? One ingenious theory ties the events of the Exodus with a massive volcanic explosion that occurred in 1628 B.C. on the island of Thera in the Mediterranean. According to this theory, the volcano caused a gigantic tidal wave that initially drained the tidal plain over which the Israelites crossed. Then, as the Egyptians followed suit, it flowed back with devastating force, trapping the charioteers. The theory that a volcano parted the Red Sea has interesting parallels with the ten plagues of Egypt—for example, connecting the casting of the land under the pall of darkness with the gigantic, sun-obscuring dust cloud accompanying the eruption. Unfortunately, this idea has a serious flaw: The date of the eruption predates the earliest acceptable date of the Exodus by nearly two centuries. Scholars continue to search for evidence that will shed light on this famous story.

Water from a Rock?

he Bible says that when the Israelites arrived at Rephidim there was no water available to them. This may have been because the Amalekites controlled the only spring in the area and were jealous to protect it.

The disgruntled Israelites demanded of Moses: "Give us water to drink" (Exodus 17:2). We then read of a curious action on the part of Moses. He was commanded by the Lord to take his rod and go to the rock of Horeb: "I will be standing there before you on the rock at Horeb. Strike the rock, and water will come out of it, so that the people may drink" (Exodus 17:6).

While this action may be unimaginable to the modern mind, Bedouin of times past or present would realize exactly what happened. In the desert wadis of the Sinai, the scarce rainfall filters down and collects in porous layers of limestone. These layers are exposed at the base of the mountains, but just as water deposits can eventually clog a faucet, the water cannot escape because of a thick buildup of limestone crust. Bedouin know precisely how to look for these hidden water sources.

Moses gets water from a rock.

There are accounts of this phenomenon in recent times. In the 1930s, Major C. S. Jarvis, the British Governor of the Sinai, was leading a camel expedition through a dry wadi when his men came across a trickle of water coming out of the limestone rock. Trying to dig into the ground where he thought there might be a pool of water, one of his men by mistake struck the rock instead. To everyone's surprise and delight, the hard crust fell away and out of the crevice shot a powerful stream of water.

This method of obtaining water was employed by Moses on at least one other occasion. We read that on the journey from Kadesh to Edom "Moses lifted up his hand and struck the rock twice with his staff. Water came out abundantly, and the congregation and their livestock drank" (Numbers 20:11). On this occasion, Moses disobeyed by striking the rock instead of speaking to it as the Lord had commanded.

We can only speculate that the Israelites had by then learned of this means of obtaining water in the desert. Perhaps God had intended to perform a miracle by having Moses speak to the rock instead of strike it. In any event, Moses' disobedience at Kadesh cost him dearly. He was denied the opportunity to personally lead the children of Israel into the Promised Land.

The Language of the Ten Commandments

As the eminent Egyptologist and archaeologist Flinders Petrie was excavating the site of Serabit el-Khadem, he found fragments of stone tablets along with a statue of a crouching figure. Both had strange markings on them, which neither Petrie nor any of the other Egyptologists present could decipher. He dated the inscriptions to around 1500 B.C.

Petrie realized that, since the writing was different from Egyptian hieroglyphics, it must have been the product of foreign workers hired by the Egyptians. But from where had these workers come? Petrie concluded they must have come from nearby Canaan.

Petrie's theory ran contrary to the "assured results" of the critical scholarship of the day, which held that writing did not appear in Canaan until around the ninth century B.C., some 600 years later than the date Petrie assigned to his inscriptions. For such scholars the story of Moses writing down the law at Sinai was an impossibility because the Canaanites did not possess their own language at that early date.

The only way to conclusively determine whether Petrie's inscriptions were of Canaanite origin was to decipher them. Unfortunately, despite the efforts of paleographers around the world, no one was able to translate them. However, one scholar, the brilliant Egyptologist Sir Alan Gardiner, managed to decipher one phrase of the text, which read "(dedicated) to (the goddess) Baalath."

This was all of the text that Gardiner was able to read, but it provided an important clue. Baalath was a female deity who was venerated in the seaport of Byblos in northern Syria. From the inscriptions, it was clear that the temple at Serabit el-Khadem was dedicated to the goddess Baalath.

The Egyptians called her by another name—Hathor. The appearance at Serabit el-Khadem of the Canaanite and Phoenician Baalath meant that laborers from those regions were working at the temple.

A crucial clue had appeared establishing that the people of Canaan possessed written language centuries earlier than many scholars had thought. They would not make the full importance of the discovery known until 30 years later, six years after Flinders Petrie's death. In 1948, archaeologists finally managed to decipher the Serabit el-Khadem texts in their entirety. What they discovered was the ancestor of our alphabet. Up until the time of its development, there were two primary modes of written language in the ancient Near East, Egyptian hieroglyphics and languages written in the cuneiform style.

The language of the Serabit el-Khadem texts is called "West Semitic" by scholars. The Greeks adapted the West Semitic alphabet in the ninth century B.C., and from there it was passed to Rome, which spread it throughout the Western world.

The discovery and deciphering of the texts at Serabit el-Khadem have lent new credibility to the divine instructions given to Moses after the defeat of the Amalekites at Rephidim: "Write this on a scroll as something to be remembered" (Exodus 17:14).

The Roman Moses

he location of the traditional site of Mount Sinai is well known to students of the Bible and to tourists visiting the Sinai peninsula. However, few may be aware of the curious story about a Roman emperor obsessed with his own visionary role as the new Moses, and how he identified the site that came to be known as the Sinai of old.

After the biblical record of the events at Mount Sinai, there are no later references in the Bible or in ancient Jewish literature that shed further light on its location. Beginning in the second century A.D., however, Christian monks began settling in southern Sinai. These hermits attempted to identify the route of the Exodus and the exact site of Mount Sinai. Two sites were suggested at this early date: Jebel Sirbal, near the oasis of Firan, or Jebel Musa, 25 miles farther south near the tip of the Sinai peninsula.

Jebel Musa came to predominate, largely due to the presence of the Monastery of Saint Catherine at the foot of the mountain. The Roman Emperor Constantine built the monastery in the fourth century to commemorate what he believed to be Mount Sinai of the Bible.

The story of how Constantine arrived at this conclusion is a rather curious one. The mystical side of the emperor who Christianized the Roman Empire can be traced back to the famous battle at Milvian Bridge outside Rome. Apparently, Constantine placed so much confidence in his visions and dreams that he often based his decisions accordingly. As the story goes, Constantine and his troops witnessed the sign of the cross in the heavens, along with the words, "By this sign conquer."

Constantine was profoundly affected by this vision, which seemed to predict success on the battlefield. He began to think of himself as a new Moses who was destined to lead the Roman Empire to new heights of glory. Before entering into battle he would retreat with his advisors into a special tent constructed in the form of a cross which he, like Moses, placed "outside the camp." Inside the tent, he would await "divine counsel."

Sinai mountains where Moses received the commandments.

The early church historian Eusebius described what happened in the tent: "And making earnest supplications to God, he was always honored after a little while with a manifestation of His [God's] presence. And then, as if moved by a divine impulse, he would rush from the tent, and suddenly give orders to his army to move at once and without delay, and on the instant to draw their swords. On this they would immediately commence the attack, fight vigorously... and raise trophies of victory over their enemies" (*Life of Constantine,* II. 12).

Eusebius relates how these "divine impulses" came to dominate Constantine's life, noting that "a thousand such acts as these were familiarly and habitually done." After becoming Emperor in A.D. 324, Constantine ordered construction of churches throughout the Holy Land to commemorate biblical events, in part as penance for the deaths of his wife Fausta and his son Crispus, whom his army executed at his command.

Constantine sent his 80-year-old mother to the Holy Land, charged with the task of locating the sites he had "foreseen" in his visions. In Jerusalem and Bethlehem, her task was made easier in that the exact location of the sites she sought had been preserved by an unbroken chain of historical records stretching back to the time of Christ.

However, in the deserts of Sinai there was little to check her imagination as she sought to determine where Mount Sinai was located. Perhaps bewildered by the vast possibilities offered by the expanse of the Sinai, she accepted the mountain suggested to her by monks living in the area. There, at the foot of Jebel Musa, she built a small chapel, which was enlarged to its present dimensions by the Emperor Justinian in A.D. 527.

In Search of Sinai

 n the spring of 1904, archaeologist Flinders Petrie set out with a long camel caravan from the Egyptian city of Suez to the Sinai peninsula. He was accompanied by a small army of scholars, surveyors, and Egyptologists.

Petrie was on a historic quest, to find the route that the Israelites took out of Egypt on their way to Mount Sinai. According to the Bible, "about 600,000 men on foot, besides children" (Exodus 12:37) led by Moses journeyed into the desert after crossing the Red Sea. However, since few of the place names mentioned in the biblical text have been definitively identified, scholars are divided as to the route they took.

One possibility was a northern route that follows the Mediterranean coast up to Canaan. It was the shortest and most logical route, which would have taken them through the territory of the Philistines. But the Bible specifically states that the Israelites did not take that route: "When Pharaoh let the people go, God did not lead them by the way of the land of the Philistines, although that was nearer" (Exodus 13:17).

The reason is given in the text. God thought, "If the people face war, they may change their minds and return to Egypt" (Exodus 13:17). Until recent times, this reference to war puzzled scholars. After all, would not this northern route be the quickest way for the Israelites to escape into Canaan?

Archaeological excavations along the Sinai coast have provided the reason the Israelites were warned against going in that direction. The route has been shown to be studded with Egyptian military fortifications. By going that way, the Israelites would have walked right into a trap.

Another possibility for the route of the Exodus would have been one of two trade routes leading through the Sinai. One of these led eastward across the desert, avoiding the southern mountains, in the direction of Beersheba. Some of those who suggest that the Israelites took this route point to a massive yellowish mountain called Jebel Yeleq as the possible Mount Sinai of the Bible. Another route went in a more easterly direction toward Ezion-Geber at the head of the Gulf of Aqaba.

Both "central" routes were virtually without water sources. They were frequented by caravan traders who carried sufficient supplies of food and water with them and who were conditioned to traveling long distances. These routes would hardly have been suitable for a slow-moving mass of people sorely dependent upon regular and copious water supplies.

For these reasons, many scholars favor what is called the "traditional" route of the Exodus. It is this route that Petrie and his caravan attempted to trace as they followed an ancient trail that led to the Sinai mountains.

Most Israelites left Egypt on foot.

Petrie had good reason to believe that the old trail was the same one that the Israelites took. In ancient times, established routes were almost never changed, remaining the same for thousands of years. The reason is they were the most convenient way of crossing whatever natural obstacles—such as mountains, rivers, and deserts—stood between the point of origin and the destination.

Petrie estimated that, on foot and traveling with their herds of sheep and goats, the Israelites could have managed around 12 miles a day. The Bible describes the first stop of the Israelites: "They went three days in the wilderness and found no water. When they came to Marah, they could not drink the water of Marah because it was bitter" (Exodus 15:22–23).

Trying to retrace this route, Petrie traveled along the ancient trail for 45 miles—or three days—before coming to a spring called Ain Hawarah by the Bedouin. The spring is little used by nomads in the area because the water is salty and sulfurous. Ain Hawarah appears to match the biblical description of the "bitter" waters of Marah, which the Israelites reached after a three-day journey.

Writing in the nineteenth century, explorer Charles Wilson writes of Ain Hawarah: "There is a stunted palm tree, or perhaps one might say a small thicket of stunted palms, shading a spring of brackish water on the slope of a ridge; and that is all." Hardly sufficient either in quantity or quality for vast numbers of thirsty Israelites.

The Bible then describes the next stop of the Israelites: "Then they came to Elim, where there were twelve springs of water and seventy palm trees; and they camped there by the water" (Exodus 15:27). In attempting to trace the Israelites' tracks, Petrie continued along the ancient route. Fifteen miles farther—about one day's march—his entourage came to Wadi Gharandel. There he found a fine oasis with shady palms and many springs, exactly as the Bible describes.

After Wadi Gharandel comes the plain of El Kaa along the shores of the Red Sea, which again corresponds with the biblical text: "The whole congregation of the Israelites set out from Elim;

and Israel came to the wilderness of Sin, which is between Elim and Sinai" (Exodus 16:1). It was here that the Israelites complained about the lack of food and were supplied with quail and manna.

From Wadi Gharandel, the ancient track led Petrie and his caravan deeper into Sinai. After rounding a sharp bend in the hills, Petrie suddenly ordered a halt. Before them stood the remains of an Egyptian temple, with stele-shaped stones carved with hieroglyphics strewn on the ground. Petrie found the name of the great Rameses II inscribed on one and immediately identified the site as Serabit el-Khadem, where for more than a thousand years the ancient Egyptians mined copper and turquoise.

Serabit el-Khadem is likely the third stop mentioned in the Bible: "They set out from the wilderness at Sin and camped at Dophkah" (Numbers 33:12). Some believe the Hebrew word "Dophkah" is related to metal or smelting operations.

Petrie's caravan came next to Feiran, which he took to be the biblical Rephidim, where the Israelites stopped next. Here the Amalekites attacked them. Through extensive surveying of the area, Petrie believed he learned the reason why. Feiran is the only water source in the entire southern part of the Sinai massif. The nomads who lived there, including the Amalekites, were dependent upon the spring for their herds. Petrie concluded that the Amalekites must have been trying to defend Wadi Feiran from the foreign invaders.

After successfully repelling the Amalekites' attack, the Israelites camped at Rephidim before continuing, unaware that some of the most momentous events of their history awaited them in the mountains towering some 25 miles distant.

The Mountain of God

he location of one of the most important events of the Old Testament—the handing down of the Ten Commandments to Moses—remains unknown. Although the traditional site of Jebel Musa has been identified with Mount Sinai since at least the fourth century, many other possibilities have also been suggested.

Some scholars believe that Mount Sinai is located not in the Sinai peninsula but in Arabia. We read in the Book of Exodus that when Moses fled Egypt, he went to the land of Midian, where he worked as a shepherd for Jethro, priest of Midian.

After spending 40 years in the desert, Moses was shepherding Jethro's flock near Horeb, "the mountain of God," when the Lord appeared to him in the burning bush (Exodus 3:1). There he is told: "When you have brought the people out of Egypt, you will worship God on this mountain" (Exodus 3:12). And indeed, after the Exodus, we find that Jethro, together with Moses' sons and wife, came to him while he was camped "near the mountain of God" (Exodus 18:5).

Some scholars have taken this to mean that the "mountain of God," known both as Horeb and Sinai, is in the former territory of the Midianites in Arabia. The reference by the Apostle Paul reinforces this view to "Mount Sinai in Arabia" in Galatians 4:25. "Arabia" here is taken to refer to what the Romans called Arabia Petraea, or Transjordan.

During the nineteenth century, an Englishman by the name of Charles Beke advanced the theory that Mount Sinai was an active volcano. The description in the biblical text appears to support that: "On the morning of the third day there was thunder and lightning, with a thick cloud over the mountain. . . . The smoke billowed up from it like smoke from a furnace, the whole mountain trembled violently, and the sound of the trumpet grew louder and louder" (Exodus 19:16, 18).

Doré woodcut of Moses with the Ten Commandments.

Beke set out for the Sinai peninsula to prove his theory and identify Sinai. He returned to England disappointed after discovering that neither Jebel Musa nor any of the other mountains of Sinai are volcanic in origin.

However, on the western side of the Arabian peninsula—the traditional territory of Midian—vast lava and ash fields provide evidence of past volcanic activity.

There are many legends among the peoples of the area involving a sacred mountain in Midian. The first-century Jewish historian Josephus mentions this sacred mountain and identifies it with Sinai. He repeatedly mentions that it was the highest mountain in the area. Accordingly, attention has focused on Jebal el-Lawz, the highest peak in northwest Arabia, where ancient

The Jebeliya Bedouin

Most present-day Bedouin of the Sinai trace their origins to the nomads of the Arabian desert. Fleeing drought, famine, and tribal conflict, they migrated in small groups to the Sinai peninsula 400 to 600 years ago.

Those extended families grew into tribes that carved out territories for themselves. The entire Sinai is divided between various Bedouin tribes. The ruling tribe owns exclusive rights to the grazing pastures, tillable land, and limited water resources.

One tribe, however—the Jebeliya—is distinct from all other Bedouin of the Sinai. They trace their lineage to the sixth century A.D. At that time a furious revolt by the Samaritans left many churches and Christian villages destroyed. After the revolt was put down, the Byzantine Emperor Justinian decided to fortify a number of monasteries in Palestine against further attacks. One of these was the small church and monastery built at the foot of Mount Sinai.

According to tradition, Justinian presented 100 Christianized Roman and Egyptian slaves, along with their wives and children, as servants to the monastery. They lived outside St. Catherine's, tending to fields and flocks. As their numbers grew Islamic authorities viewed the Christian tribes as a threat and decided to force them to convert to Islam.

Many prepared to resist. In the end, however, they yielded and renounced their faith, except for one man who prepared to throw himself over the peak. The man's wife pleaded with him to kill her and their children rather than be forced to deny their faith. The tormented man drew his sword and killed his family.

He leaped off the cliff, but survived. The tragedy so marked him that he wandered about the mountains, living with wild beasts in caves and holes. According to written accounts, at the end of his life, he appeared at the doors of the monastery, where he received Holy Communion and was ministered to by the monks before dying peacefully.

The descendants of those tribes that converted to Islam are known as the Jebeliya—"the tribes of the mountain (of Sinai)"—to this day they still tend the fields and gardens of St. Catherine's Monastery.

Midian was located. By comparison, the traditional site of Sinai, 7,400-foot-high Jebel Musa in the Sinai Peninsula, is not the highest peak in the area.

Despite this, the traditionally cited location of Sinai is not easily overturned. A location in the southern Sinai peninsula fits better with the movements of the Israelites after the Exodus as recorded in the biblical text.

In the end, it would appear that, like the events that transpired on it, the location of the mountain of God will remain hidden from mortal eyes.

The Ark of the Covenant

he Ark of the Covenant was an elaborate container that symbolized God's presence among the ancient Israelites.

The Hebrew word for "ark" can be used interchangeably to mean "box," "chest," or "coffin" and was used to describe objects as diverse as the coffin of Joseph and the collection box in the temple. The word "covenant" refers to the original purpose of the Ark as a container for the Ten Commandments.

The Ark was constructed while the Israelites resided at Mount Sinai. After the original tablets of the law were broken by Moses because of the Israelites' idolatry, he made it out of acacia wood as a container for the new tablets. The Ark was a rectangular-shaped box approximately four feet long, two-and-a-half feet wide, and two-and-a-half feet deep. It was designed with built-in handles for portability and was carried only by priests.

During the wanderings of the Israelites, the Ark was kept within the tabernacle. Moses addressed the Ark as if the divine presence were within: "Whenever the Ark set out, Moses would say, 'Arise, O Lord, let your enemies be scattered, and your foes flee before you.' And whenever it came to rest, he would say, 'Return O Lord of the ten thousand thousands of Israel'" (Numbers 10:35–36).

As the powerful symbol of God's presence, the Ark was routinely taken into battle. During the period of the Judges, the sin of the wicked sons of Eli led to the defeat of the Israelites by the Philistines. The Ark was captured by their mortal enemies.

This led to a series of adventures in which the Ark was passed from one Philistine city to another, bringing calamity to each one in turn. The Ark was placed in the temple of the Philistine god Dagon in Ashdod, after which we read: "When the people of Ashdod rose early the next day, there was Dagon, fallen on his face to the ground before the Ark of the Lord. So they took Dagon and put him back in his place. But when they rose early on the next morning, Dagon had fallen on his face to the ground before the Ark of the Lord, and the head of Dagon and both his hands were lying cut off upon the threshold; only the trunk of Dagon was left to him" (1 Samuel 5:3–4).

This was a sign of things to come, for we then read: "The hand of the Lord was heavy upon the people of Ashdod, and he terrified them and struck them with tumors" (1 Samuel 5:6). By this time the inhabitants of Ashdod had quite enough of the Ark and passed it on to the next Philistine city. Once again, its inhabitants were tormented by tumors, until finally they decided to send it back to the Israelites.

The Hebrews rejoiced to see the Ark returning to them. It was pulled across the fields of Bethshemesh on an ox-drawn cart. However, the sacredness and mysterious powers of

The Ark of the Covenant held the Ten Commandments.

the Ark would soon be impressed upon the Israelites. When a clan of Israelites known as the descendants of Jeconiah refused to celebrate the return of the Ark, 70 of them were struck down.

Years later, when David became king, he brought the Ark up to Jerusalem. On the way, Uzziah "reached out his hand to the Ark of God and took hold of it, for the oxen shook it. The anger of the Lord was kindled against Uzziah; and God struck him there because he reached out his hand to the Ark; and he died there beside the Ark of God" (2 Samuel 6:6–7).

We read that David was angered because the Lord struck down Uzziah, and the divine action can perhaps only be understood as emphasizing the holiness of God, before whom no man can stand. Apparently, Uzziah disregarded one very important command from God: Not to touch the Ark and respect its sanctity.

After this incident, David was reluctant to bring the Ark to Jerusalem, and for three months the Ark was entrusted to the care of Obed-edom the Gittite, during which time he and his household were greatly blessed.

David's successor, Solomon, placed the Ark within the Holy of Holies of his temple. At this point, the Ark was said to contain Aaron's rod that budded and a pot of manna, along with the Ten Commandments. Hovering over the Ark in the darkness of the Holy of Holies were two golden cherubim, their solitude disturbed only by the annual appearance of the High Priest.

Most scholars believe the Ark of the Covenant was captured or destroyed by the Babylonians when Jerusalem fell in 586 B.C. Some believe that this mysterious object was not destroyed but remains in a secret location, ready to be revealed at the ordained time.

In Search of the Biblical Manna

According to the Bible, the Israelites were nourished during their 40-year stay in the desert by food that miraculously appeared each morning on the ground: "The house of Israel called it manna. It was like coriander seed, white, and the taste of it was like wafers made with honey" (Exodus 16:31).

Students of the Bible through the centuries have sought to identify what manna was, and pilgrims to the deserts of Sinai reported seeing and ingesting substances that resembled manna. In 1823, German botanist G. Ehrenberg offered an ingenious the-

Manna: A Pilgrim's Account

The following account was written in 1483 by a German named Breitenback, identified as the Dean of Mainz, following his visit to the Sinai:

"In every valley throughout the whole region of Mount Sinai, there can still be found Bread of Heaven, which the monks and the Arabs gather, preserve, and sell to pilgrims and strangers who pass that way. This same Bread of Heaven falls about daybreak like dew or hoarfrost and hangs in beads on grass, stones, and twigs. It is sweet like honey and sticks to the teeth. We bought a lot of it."

ory as to its origin. Ehrenberg believed that the biblical manna was actually a secretion of tamarisk trees, which are found in the Sinai. The secretion is produced by two kinds of scaled insects that feed on the sap of the tamarisk.

Tamarisk sap is rich in carbohydrates but poor in nitrogen. Large quantities of the sap are consumed by the insects in order to obtain sufficient nitrogen, and the excess carbohydrate is excreted in the form of a liquid containing three kinds of sugars and a jellylike substance known as pectin. This would account for the description of manna as tasting like honey.

The secretion dries quickly in the hot desert climate, leaving sticky droplets behind, once again prompting comparison with the biblical text, which states that "when the layer of dew lifted, there on the surface of the wilderness was a fine flaky substance, as fine as frost on the ground" (Exodus 16:14).

A hundred years after Ehrenberg, a "manna expedition" to Sinai was organized by scientists from the Hebrew University in Jerusalem. After several months of investigation, the expedition brought back photographic and other evidence linking the insect secretions with the biblical manna. The scientists discovered that the secretions are approximately the size and shape of a coriander seed just as the Bible states.

The biblical text adds that the manna was white in color. Similarly, the insect secretions are initially white, but after lying on the ground they turn yellowish-brown. In tasting the secretions, the scientists reported that it resembled honey that has been left to solidify. The local Bedouin Arabs call the insect secretions from the tamarisk sap "Mann es-Sama"—meaning "Manna from Heaven." They gather it early as the Israelites did, because when the sun rises, ants and other insects find and consume it. The Israelites also found that any unconsumed manna "bred worms and became foul" overnight (Exodus 16:20).

Would this manna be sufficient to feed the Israelites? In good years, according to reports, the Bedouin of Sinai can gather up to four pounds of it per day, enough to satisfy a grown man.

While intriguing, the identification of Mann es-Sama as the biblical manna is not satisfactory. Questions remain whether it would provide sufficient nourishment over a long period of time.

Meat in the Desert

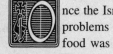nce the Israelites escaped across the Red Sea, their problems were far from over. After a month, their food was running out, and some people began to think perhaps their former life as slaves wasn't so bad after all.

The Israelites complained bitterly to Moses: "If only we had died by the hand of the Lord in the land of Egypt, when we sat by the fleshpots and ate our fill of bread; for you have brought us out into this wilderness to kill this whole assembly with hunger" (Exodus 16:3).

We then read that the Lord heard the cries of the Israelites and promised that their needs would be met immediately: "At twilight you shall eat meat, and in the morning you shall have your fill of bread; then you shall know that I am the Lord your God" (Exodus 16:8).

To supply food for well over a million men, women, and children is no simple task in a desert environment. However, the text records that in the very same evening "quails came and covered the camp," providing the people with longed-for meat (Exodus 16:13). Is there any evidence that could corroborate this incredible event?

Amazingly, there is. The great Israeli soldier and statesman Moshe Dayan spent years traversing the Sinai when Israel controlled the area militarily. Through his intimate knowledge of the area and his contacts with the Bedouin, he learned of a remarkable parallel to the biblical account.

Every autumn, birds from the northern hemisphere, including quail, migrate south. Their migration route takes them from central Europe south through Turkey. There the birds prepare to cross the Mediterranean in a single night, made necessary by the absence of an intervening land mass for the birds to rest.

The birds must cover a great distance, and maintain a high speed of 50 miles per hour. Every year, untold numbers of birds give in to the rigors of the flight and fall into the sea.

The quails approach the coast as the first rays of dawn appear on the horizon, illuminating palm trees along the shore. Spurred on by the sight, the birds drop to only a few yards above the water. Without losing speed they make for the trees and drop exhausted to the ground. There they lie in the sand, warming themselves in the autumn sun.

Many do not get to complete their migration. The local Bedouin eagerly await the arrival of the quail. Fences of fish-netting are strung along the shore, trapping some of the fatigued birds as they prepared to land.

On their return trip in the spring, the surviving birds faced another threat as they crossed the Red Sea and lighted on the shores to gather their strength to continue their flight over the mountains of Sinai. The first-century Jewish historian Josephus describes the Bedouin catching the exhausted quails by hand.

Through the generations, Bedouin have been so successful at trapping the helpless, depleted quail that most of the vast migration flights have disappeared. In biblical times their numbers were likely far greater—perhaps even enough to provide flesh for the multitudes of Israelites to enjoy.

Ancient Israel
Did Ancient Israel Exist?

eferences to ancient Israel outside the Bible are few. One mention that has been of considerable interest to scholars is an inscription found in an Egyptian temple at the end of the last century. It sheds light on one of the most important events in Israel's early history.

The date of the Exodus and the Israelites' conquest of Canaan has been fiercely debated among scholars. One popular theory is that the biblical portrayal is an exaggerated account of what was actually a gradual process during which the Israelites emerged from peoples indigenous to Canaan.

According to this theory, the dramatic stories of the conquest of Jericho and other cities are merely religiously motivated fables with little historical basis. The time when the development of the Israelite nation supposedly took place is the middle of the twelfth century B.C.—around 1150 B.C. That is more than 200 years later than the Bible says the conquest of Canaan took place.

An example of a stela.

In 1896, the great Egyptologist Flinders Petrie was excavating in the mortuary temple of Pharaoh Merneptah in Thebes when he discovered what has become known as the Merneptah Stela. A stela is a cut, standing stone with writing on it used in ancient times to chronicle important events in the reign of a king or pharaoh.

The Merneptah Stela preserves what is the most important mention of Israel outside the Bible and the only mention of Israel in Egyptian records. The stela is, in fact, a poetic eulogy to Merneptah, who ruled after Rameses the Great, from 1212 B.C. to 1202 B.C. At the end of the poem is a record of a military campaign into Canaan by Merneptah around 1210 B.C. It is here that we find the citation: "Israel is laid waste, its seed is not."

This text poses a problem for the so-called gradual emergence theory, for it suggests that Israel was already a recognizable entity by 1210 B.C. instead of 1150 B.C. or later. Accordingly, the Merneptah Stela has been carefully analyzed by scholars in an attempt to harmonize it with the gradual emergence theory. It has been suggested that the word "Israel" actually refers to "Jezreel," the valley in the north of the country, or perhaps to the Libyans—"the wearers of the side lock."

These alternative renderings have not met with widespread acceptance. The word for Israel is accompanied in the Merneptah Stela with a special hieroglyphic indicator for people, not a geographic feature, such as a valley. The presence of Israel in a list of Canaanite peoples argues against identifying it with Libya.

Attention has also focused on the meaning of the word "seed" as it appears in the stela. There are only two possibilities, "grain" or "offspring," but a comparison with the use of the same term in other Egyptian texts affirms that it refers to grain.

It would be unwise to attempt to draw too much from this overly scrutinized text. The evidence does show that, by the late thirteenth century B.C., a nation named Israel existed, and was an important enough military power to be mentioned in the stela.

It also seems clear by the reference to grain that the Israelites were primarily agrarian. The biblical text supports the fact that during this period the Israelites did not occupy fortified city-states but were primarily tillers of the soil. Grain storage pits are common to the hill country sites that they occupied.

The examination of teeth from tombs of the period also indicates that grain was a primary food source. The worn state of the teeth is due to the fact that stone mills were used to grind the grain, which would therefore contain minute particles of stone.

The debate over the date of the Exodus and the conquest of Canaan continues, and this latest research will surely give biblical scholars something more to chew on.

When Did the Walls of Jericho Collapse?

 t was from the east that the Israelites converged upon Jericho after camping "at Gilgal on the east border of Jericho" (Joshua 4:19). According to the biblical account, the Israelites marched around the city once a day for six days. On the seventh day, they encircled the city seven times, after which they blew their trumpets and shouted. The Bible records that the walls collapsed, and the Israelites rushed in and conquered the city.

Several major archaeological excavations of Jericho have been undertaken in the past century, each hoping to uncover some evidence related to the biblical story. In 1907 and 1909, an Austro-German team uncovered the base of the city and what appeared to be massive piles of bricks. It would take another half a century before those findings would be identified.

English archaeologist John Garstang worked at the site from 1930 to 1936 and stunned the scholarly world by announcing that the walls of Jericho had indeed fallen, sometime before 1400 B.C. However, archaeology was still in its infancy in Garstang's day (it is considered a "young" science even today), and by modern standards his techniques were crude.

Mound covering Jericho.

Another English archaeologist, Dame Kathleen Kenyon, overturned Garstang's conclusions after excavating at Jericho between 1952 and 1958. Kenyon determined that the piles of bricks were from a city wall that had collapsed when the city was destroyed. She dismayed Bible enthusiasts by concluding that this destruction occurred at the end of the Middle Bronze Age, around 1550 B.C.—centuries before the generally accepted date for the Israelites' arrival into Canaan. Since the walls had fallen long before Joshua's time, there was, in effect, no city for the Israelites to conquer.

Kenyon's conclusions had a significant influence on biblical studies for decades, as skeptics used them as a prime example of what they claimed was the historical unreliability of the Bible. Nevertheless, the question of the walls of Jericho continued to dog scholars, some of whom turned their critical attention to Kenyon herself. She died in 1978 without having ever published a formal excavation report, a regrettable omission.

In Kenyon's case, a reexamination of her original data has led some scholars to question her conclusions. Clearly, she found evidence of massive destruction: walls and floors blackened by fire, and rooms filled with fallen bricks, burnt timbers, and debris. Yet when did this destruction occur?

The likely answer came when scientists carbon-dated a piece of charcoal from the debris layer to 1410 B.C., with a margin of error of plus or minus 40 years. This date coincided with other evidence ignored by Kenyon, such as Garstang's discovery of a continuous sequence of Egyptian scarabs (decorative beetle-shaped carvings) at the site.

Garstang also recorded large amounts of pottery fragments dating to the same period. If the destruction of the walls of Jericho actually occurred around 1400 B.C., this would support the traditional date of the fall of Jericho indicated by the Bible.

This latest evaluation of the evidence from excavations at Jericho remains hotly debated among archaeologists, and only time will tell whether Kenyon's conclusions will stand up—or collapse like the walls of Jericho.

The Parting of the Jordan

fter Hebrew spies returned from Jericho, the Israelites prepared to cross the Jordan River and enter the Promised Land. Even in biblical times, before modern irrigation siphoned off much of its water, the Jordan scarcely deserved to be called a river during much of the year.

However, we are told that "the Jordan overflows all its banks throughout the time of harvest" (Joshua 3:15). This is the grain harvest in late spring, when the snows of Mount Hermon at the headwaters of the Jordan begin to melt. The river is transformed into a swift, churning tide that greatly enlarges its banks, making it impossible to cross.

Even in modern times, the river has proved difficult to manage. In 1917, on its way to attack Amman, the British army lost many soldiers to the swift currents before it managed to secure guide ropes across the river.

Was it a miracle that enabled the Israelites to cross? As the priests bearing the Ark of the Covenant came to the Jordan, "the waters flowing from above stood still, rising up in a single heap far off at Adam, the city that is beside Zarethan, while those flowing toward the sea of the Arabah, the Dead Sea, were wholly cut off. Then the people crossed over opposite Jericho" (Joshua 3:16).

The biblical account of the crossing of the Jordan is often assumed to be fanciful. There is, however, interesting historical data that lends some credibility to the story. Scholars have discovered that, over the past 2,000 years, the region has experienced at least 30 earthquakes. Interestingly, resulting mud slides caused temporary damming of the Jordan River ten different times.

The most recent of these occurred in 1927 at a ford known as al-Damiyeh, some 25 miles upstream. An earthquake loosened great masses of earth from overhanging cliffs that fell into the river and choked the narrow ford. The flow of water was completely stopped for 21 hours.

The river had also been stopped up by an earthquake three years earlier, in 1924, and in 1906. In the latter case, the river bed at the lower reaches of the Jordan was completely dry for 24 hours.

There is little doubt that the occurrence of an earthquake just as the Israelites were preparing to cross the Jordan is highly remarkable. But whether labeled as a coincidence by skeptics, or as a miracle through the eyes of faithful, the possibility cannot be discounted.

Did Samson Destroy the Temple?

he tragic biblical account of Samson's life and death is a powerful story. After Delilah betrayed Samson, the Philistines gouged out his eyes and took him to Gaza, where he was imprisoned and forced to grind grain for his enemies.

Archaeological evidence shows that the Philistines routinely interred prisoners in "grinding houses," where they were forced

Von Carolsfeld's rendering of Samson destroying the Temple.

to perform what was one of the most time-consuming and tedious tasks of antiquity, that of milling flour. In the home, women performed this task using a hand-held pestle and a mortar placed in the lap.

Grinding houses provided flour for the elite of Philistine society. The mills they used consisted of large stones with protruding wooden shanks on either side set on a flat stone. Human labor would rotate the top stone, thus grinding the grain against the bottom stone. Limestone was used, but the superior mills were made of basalt, an extremely hard volcanic rock found in northern Israel.

According to the biblical text, Samson was brought forth to entertain the assembled Philistines. Once in their company, he asked to be guided to two pillars in the center of the building so he could lean against them. Then we read: "He strained with all his might; and the house fell on the lords and all the people who were in it. So those he killed at his death were more than those he had killed during his life" (Judges 16:30).

Is it possible that such a thing could have happened? Archaeological excavation of the Philistine cities gives evidence related to the biblical story. Philistine temples have been uncovered at Tel Qasile in northern Tel Aviv, and at Tel Miqne, the ancient Ekron. Interestingly, the roofs of both temples were supported by twin central pillars made of wood resting on stone support bases. The pillars were about six feet apart, making it theoretically possible for them to be dislodged, collapsing the roof.

It would take a person of superhuman strength to accomplish such a feat, which certainly fits the description of Samson before he was compromised by Delilah. The Bible states that his hair, which was the source of his might before the Philistines cut it off, began to grow back in prison.

The Daring Capture of Jerusalem

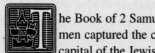 he Book of 2 Samuel tells the story of how David's men captured the city of Jerusalem and made it the capital of the Jewish kingdom. The Jebusites inhabited the city, and were so confident of their position that they taunted the Israelites: "You will not come in here, even the blind and the lame will turn you back" (2 Samuel 5:6).

Scholars are divided as to the meaning of the Hebrew word *tsinnor,* which is translated "water shaft" in the following passage: "Nevertheless David took the stronghold of Zion, which is now the city of David. David had said on that day, 'Whoever would strike down the Jebusites, let him get up the water shaft (*tsinnor*) to attack the lame and the blind, those whom David hates'" (2 Samuel 5:7–8). Since the word tsinnor only occurs one other time in the Bible, a number of possibilities for its meaning have been suggested, including various weapons or parts of the defenses of the city.

Most translations of the Bible, however, translate *tsinnor* as a shaft, conduit, or channel used for carrying water. This interpretation has been supported by the discovery of an ancient water shaft that served the Jebusite city and would have been an ideal means for entering the city by stealth. The shaft, now named after the British explorer Charles Warren who discovered it in the nineteenth century, brought water from the Gihon Spring inside the city walls.

In ancient times, a city deprived of its water supply could not withstand a siege for long. The Jebusites sought to protect their water supply by sealing the original entrance to the Gihon Spring and diverting the water to a rock-cut tunnel leading under the city walls. The tunnel then connected with a 40-foot vertical shaft from which water could be drawn and carried into the city.

The Jebusite city occupied a small, highly defensible knoll extending south from the Turkish walls of Jerusalem. Surrounded by the steep hillsides of the Kidron and Tyropoeon valleys the city would have presented a challenge to any invaders.

Hence the bold confidence of the Jebusites, who seemingly did not consider the possibility that the secret of their concealed water system had been detected by the Israelites. Apparently, the Israelite commander Joab uncovered the original entrance to the spring during the night. He and his men then crept through the channel and ascended Warren's Shaft. Once inside the city, they could have opened the city gates to allow the rest of the army to swarm in and capture it.

To remove any doubt as to the feasibility of entering the city this way, a group of archaeologists traced the likely steps of Joab and his men. Without using special climbing equipment, they were able to scale Warren's Shaft unaided, just as Joab and his men probably did three thousand years ago.

The Twenty-Four Carat Temple

he biblical depiction of the vast quantities of gold used in King Solomon's Temple staggers the Western mind, causing some scholars to label it a gross exaggeration.

We read that "Solomon overlaid the inside of the [Temple] with pure gold, then he drew chains of gold across, in front of the inner sanctuary, and overlaid it with gold. Next he overlaid the whole [Temple] with gold, in order that the whole house might be perfect" (1 Kings 6:21–22). Some biblical commentaries allow that perhaps selected parts of the temple, such as the altar, could have been gold-plated. Others suggest that it was actually gold paint applied to the walls. Clearly, they say, the so-called Golden Temple was a tale that grew with the telling.

The list of sacred objects and utensils crafted with gold seems endless: "King Solomon made large shields of beaten gold; six hundred shekels of gold went into each large shield. He made three hundred shields of beaten gold, three minas of gold went into each shield. . . . The king also made a great ivory throne, and overlaid it with the finest gold. . . . All King Solomon's drinking vessels were of gold, and all the vessels of the House of the Forest of Lebanon were of pure gold;

Solomon's temple.

none were of silver—it was not considered as anything in the days of Solomon" (1 Kings 10:16–18, 21).

To the modern mind, such lavish use of gold may seem garish. By comparing the biblical depiction of King Solomon's wealth with that of the kings of neighboring cultures, we find his use of gold to be remarkably similar to his contemporaries.

Perhaps the least unusual is the claim that all of Solomon's tableware was pure gold. Examples of golden tableware have been found throughout the ancient Near East. Between 1927 and 1931, Sir Leonard Woolley, excavator of Ur, found many specimens of pure gold in his excavation of the Royal Cemetery.

Neither is the description of Solomon's golden throne implausible. Ancient potentates prized furniture made of precious metal, as proved by the carved wooden chairs plated with gold found in the tomb of Pharaoh Tutankhamen in Upper Egypt. Babylonian cuneiform documents record gifts of golden furniture to the gods and goddesses or from one king to another.

The Bible describes Solomon's throne as composed of both ivory and gold: "The King also made a great ivory throne and overlaid it with the finest gold" (1 Kings 10:18). The similar use of gold-overlaid ivory in furniture has been discovered at the ancient Assyrian palaces at Ninevah. Thousands of ivory pieces were found, some with fragments of gold foil still sticking to them. When the Babylonians and the Medes sacked the city, they smashed the ivory furniture, tearing off the gold.

Since gold is not strong enough to withstand an arrow or a blow from an ax, the five hundred shields of hammered gold mentioned in the biblical text would have been of little practical use. Sir Leonard Woolley uncovered similar artifacts at Ur, including a golden helmet, which, although of superb construction, would have been a hazard when used.

Finally, the sheer quantity of gold mentioned in the text is almost inconceivable to the modern mind. Solomon's golden shields weighed nearly two tons; the Queen of Sheba presented Solomon with a gift of 120 talents of gold (9,000 pounds, or four-and-a-half tons of gold); and Hiram, king of Tyre, presented Solomon with a similar amount.

As astounding as these figures may be, they are not unusual for the ancient Near East, where we find records of gifts of gold that exceed those mentioned in the biblical account. When the Assyrian king Tiglath-pileser III subjugated Tyre in 730 B.C., he received a tribute of 150 talents of gold. In Egypt, Thutmos III presented a gift of 13.5 tons of gold to the temple of Amun at Karnak.

All this underscores the vast quantities of gold that must have been circulating in the ancient world. Most of it has disappeared from history. Greek sources confirm that when Alexander the Great conquered Persia, he found almost 7,000 tons of gold.

Where did all this gold come from? There are no significant sources of gold in Israel. The Egyptians mined gold at the headwaters of the Nile, and the Queen of Sheba likely used gold mines in western Arabia. The mention in the biblical text of "gold of Ophir" (1Kings 10:11) remains a puzzle to scholars. Some think it refers to the mines of western Arabia, while others suggest more distant sites, such as India or the Horn of Africa.

The Color Purple

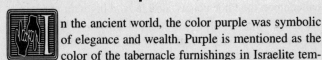 n the ancient world, the color purple was symbolic of elegance and wealth. Purple is mentioned as the color of the tabernacle furnishings in Israelite temples, and priests were commanded to have purple in their garments. In Proverbs, a good wife was worthy of being clothed in purple. In the New Testament parable of the rich man and Lazarus, the rich man "was dressed in purple and fine linen" (Luke 16:19). Jesus was mockingly honored as a king and

clothed in a purple robe at his trial (Mark 15:17). In the Book of Acts, Lydia, a highly esteemed Christian woman, is described as a "dealer in purple" (Acts 16:14).

The colorfast purple dye was associated with wealth because it was extremely costly to obtain. In ancient times, the dye had one source: the murex shell or mollusk, which is native to the eastern Mediterranean. Each murex contains only a pinprick amount of the dye, which must be laboriously removed by hand. In Capernaum, on the shores of the sea of Galilee, a murex production facility was excavated, and a thin needle used to extract the dye was found. Thousands of murex mollusks are required to produce even a small amount of dye, and heaps of discarded shells can be seen at various sites along the coastline.

The Phoenicians maintained a monopoly on murex throughout ancient times. The names "Canaan" and "Phoenician" are both related to the color purple. Some scholars think "Canaan" is derived from the Akkadian word for "red-purple." Similarly, the Greeks named Phoenicia after their word for the color purple.

When King Solomon was preparing to build a temple he called upon the Phoenicians' skill in working with murex dye. He asked King Huram of Tyre to send artisans skilled in working with "purple, crimson, and blue fabrics" (2 Chronicles 2:7). In response, Huram sent one Huram-abi, who did the work Solomon requested (2 Chronicles 2:13, 14).

In the 1970s, the ancient Phoenician site of Zarephath (modern Sarafand in Lebanon) was excavated. Zarephath was an important site for the production of murex dye. A vat containing purple sediment was uncovered, as well as large numbers of discarded murex mollusks. A similar vat was found at the archaeological site of Dor on the Mediterranean coast in Israel. These vats were used to immerse cloth for dying. Waterproof and permanent, the dye was superior to vegetable-based colors.

Murex dye continued to be highly prized until less costly substitutes were developed. However, the value of the murex dye is still reflected in the use of colors such as royal blue to signify dignity and authority.

The Moabite Version of a Biblical Story

An extraordinary inscription on what is called the Moabite Stone sheds light on a little known corner of biblical history. The inscription is the longest monumental record found in Palestine. It begins with the introduction: "I am Mesha, son of Chemosh[it], king of Moab, the Dibonite."

Mesha was a contemporary of Jehoshaphat (872–848 B.C.), king of the southern kingdom of Judah, and Jehoram (852–841 B.C.), king of the northern kingdom of Israel. Mesha ruled the kingdom of Moab, east of the Dead Sea. After the death of Ahab he revolts against his successor, Jehoram (2 Kings 3). This is the only biblical text that mentions Mesha.

Attacking Mesha's forces from the south, Jehoram joins Jehoshaphat and the King of Edom in putting down the revolt. The Moabite forces are routed, and many towns destroyed as the grip closes in around Mesha's remaining forces. When he sees that he is surrounded, Mesha sacrifices his firstborn son to the Moabite god Chemosh, causing the Israelites to withdraw.

The revolt must have taken place between 852 and 848 B.C., when both Jehoram and Jehoshaphat were ruling. Mesha recorded his version of the same event on a stone slab measuring three feet high and two feet wide. Unfortunately, the stela was smashed, but not before an imprint of the inscription had been made. Furthermore, approximately two-thirds of the pieces were eventually recovered, permitting it to be reconstructed.

The message it bears is written in the Moabite language, which is almost identical to Hebrew, and consists of 34 lines. The inscription gives Mesha's version of events, being careful to sidestep the matter of his defeat at the hands of Jehoram, Jehoshaphat, and the king of Edom. Mesha's version describes a successful revolt and the recapturing of Moabite territory, being careful to give credit to Chemosh, the national god of Moab.

The inscription also avoids mention of Jehoram's successful attack from the south. Instead, it tells of the conquest of the town of Nebo and the spoils of war Mesha acquired, including the "altar-hearths of Yahweh." Here is the earliest mention of the full name of Yahweh, the God of the Israelites, outside the Bible. Chemosh appears on the inscription 11 times.

The Moabite Stone also states: "And I built . . . the temple of Baal Meon, and I established there . . . the sheep of the land." The mention of sheep refers to the primary occupation of the Moabites, also mentioned in the Bible: "Now King Mesha of Moab was a sheep breeder, who used to deliver to the king of Israel one hundred thousand rams" (2 Kings 3:4).

Sacrifice on the City Wall

he Book of 2 Kings relates a baffling incident in the story of the revolt of King Mesha of Moab against an alliance led by King Jehoram of Israel.

When the battle went against Mesha, we read: "Then he took his firstborn son who was to succeed him, and offered him as a burnt offering on the wall. And great wrath came upon Israel, so they withdrew from him and returned to their own land" (2 Kings 3:27).

The act of sacrificing his own son, the crown prince, on the walls of the city apparently achieved what Mesha intended. The Israelite forces withdrew, and for the next two centuries Moab remained independent.

Scholars have been at a loss to explain this shocking action on the part of King Mesha. Recent discoveries, however, have shed light on the religious and cultural atmosphere in which the sacrifice of Mesha's son took place.

A cuneiform tablet from the city of Ugarit in Syria reveals that Mesha's sacrifice of his son was not unique. Such actions were considered religious acts, intended to obtain the protection of the Canaanite god Baal.

The Ugaritic text states that when an enemy attacks the walls of the city, the following promise is to be made to Baal: "We shall sacrifice a bull to thee, O Baal, A votive-pledge we shall fulfill: A firstborn, Baal, we shall sacrifice, A child we shall fulfill...." The text then promises that Baal will answer the prayers of the inhabitants of the city and drive the enemy away.

The Phoenicians, who also worshiped Baal, founded the colony of Carthage in north Africa. Writing around 50 B.C., Roman historian Diodorus of Sicily describes a military campaign that went against the Carthaginians. Diodorus relates that, when they saw the enemy besieging the walls of their city, "they selected of the noblest children and sacrificed them publicly."

Another Roman historian, Rufus, reports that a similar incident occurred when Alexander the Great was besieging the Phoenician city of Tyre. It was suggested that a freeborn boy be sacrificed, but in this instance, the elders of the city opposed the idea. Despite such exceptions, Phoenician historian Sanchuniaton attests to the practice of sacrificing children to appease their high god in times of great danger or distress.

The biblical story simply relates that, upon seeing Mesha's sacrificed son, "great wrath came upon Israel, so they withdrew from him and returned to their own country" (2 Kings 3:27). The "great wrath" can be taken to mean a traumatic response, in this case the result of witnessing the act of human sacrifice. The Israelites were likely so sickened by the sight that they no longer had the will to fight.

The Israelite alliance that came against Moab was probably not the first army to be turned away by the sight of persons—

often children—being sacrificed. The Ugaritic text, in offering assurances that the ploy would work, apparently was based on experience.

The biblical story of King Mesha sacrificing his son illuminates the sharply contrasted ethical standards of Israelite and Canaanite religions.

Alas, Babylon

n the Book of Jeremiah (50:35–36, 38), we read a harsh denunciation of Babylon and a prediction of its doom because of its obsession with the worship of false gods:

> "A sword against the Chaldeans, says the Lord,
>   and against the inhabitants of Babylon,
>   and against her officials and her sages!
> A sword against the diviners,
>   so that they may become fools!
> A sword against her warriors,
>   so they may be destroyed!...
> A drought against her waters,
>   that they may be dried up!
> For it is a land of images,
>   and they go mad over idols."

In 605 B.C., Nebuchadnezzar became king of Babylon, reigning for 43 years. Rather than boast about his prowess on the battlefield, as did the militant Assyrians before him, Nebuchadnezzar preferred instead to record the many temples that he built in Babylon. Archaeology confirms the worship of idols in Babylon, and that Nebuchadnezzar built many temples for them.

One of these gods, Marduk, is known as Bel in the Bible. God, speaking through the prophet Jeremiah, says: "I will punish Bel in Babylon, and make him disgorge what he has swallowed. The nations shall no longer stream to him; the wall of Babylon has fallen" (Jeremiah 51:44).

Babylon was among the largest and most important cities of ancient Mesopotamia. In classical times, its renowned Hanging Gardens were listed among the Seven Wonders of the Ancient World. The Greek historian Herodotus reportedly visited the city in 460 B.C., claiming that it "surpasses in splendor any city of the known world."

The fall of Babylon.

Inside the massive walls were more than a thousand temples and religious structures that served a population of nearly 100,000. One ancient inscription provides the details: "Altogether there are in Babylon 53 temples of the chief gods, 55 chapels of Marduk, 300 chapels of earthly deities, 600 for the heavenly deities, 180 altars for the goddess Ishtar, 180 for the gods Nergal and Adad, and 12 other altars for different gods."

The most prominent temple in Babylon was Esagila ("the temple that raises its head"), in which Marduk, the patron god of Babylon, dwelled. The huge temple enclosure contained at least 50 shrines. Excavators found more than 6,000 figures and figurines at the site, attesting to Jeremiah's comment that the city was "mad over idols."

Next to Esagila was the great ziggurat named Etemenanki ("the foundation house of heaven and earth"). Thought to be similar to the Tower of Babel, the stepped, pyramid-shaped temple was nearly 300 feet square and rose nearly 300 feet high.

So confident were the Babylonians of their fortifications that they named the city's famous processional way Aibur-shabu, which means "the enemy shall never pass here." The city was surrounded by three massive concentric walls as much as 11 miles in circumference. The space between them was wide enough for Herodotus' four-horse chariot to turn around. As an added precaution, the outermost wall formed the scarp of a moat that was up to 330 feet wide. The mighty kingdom of Babylon gradually entered a period of internal decline. Despite its elaborate defensive fortifications, the city was captured without a struggle in 539 B.C. by the Persians under Cyrus the Great. Thus ended Babylon's dominant role in the ancient Near East.

The city was still impressive in the days of Herodotus, and more than a century later, in 323 B.C., Alexander the Great was sufficiently enchanted with Babylon to embark upon an ambitious scheme to rebuild it. Those plans were cut short, however, when Alexander succumbed to fever in the city that same year, thus sealing its fate. By 200 B.C., Babylon lay deserted.

THE PROPHETIC BOOKS
Fire and Rain

rouble visited the kingdom of Israel when their king, Ahab, married a Sidonian princess by the name of Jezebel. The meaning of her name, "Baal is the prince," foreshadows the fierce struggle that her reign would initiate between the god Baal and Yahweh, the God of the Israelites.

Jezebel sought to replace the prophets in Israel with prophets of Baal and his consort Asherah. Baal's name means "lord" or "owner," and he was the supreme deity of Canaan and worshiped by the Phoenicians, the Philistines, and other peoples of the region. Hence the various derivatives of Baal mentioned in the Bible, including the Philistine Baal-Zebub, or "lord of the flies" (or "lord of the prince"); the Moabite Baal-Meon, or "lord of the residence"; and Baal-Gad, "the lord of Gad" of Lebanon.

Baal was a storm-god who was believed to send the rains in their seasons. His entourage included rain clouds, and lightning was his weapon. Baal worship was a great temptation for the water-poor land of Israel. Unlike the great river cultures of Egypt and Mesopotamia, Israel had no constant supply of water and was thus dependent upon the winter rains to sustain its crops.

In return for supplying rain, Baal was thought to demand submission in the form of human sacrifice. In the Bible, this form of sacrifice is termed "to pass through the fire." As the phrase suggests, the victims were burned alive, and such sacrifice was given as a primary cause for the fall of the kingdom of Israel: "They made their sons and their daughters pass through fire; they used divination and augury; and they sold themselves to do evil in the sight of the Lord" (2 Kings 17:17).

The degradation that Baal worship threatened to bring upon Israel prompted the prophet Elijah to confront the prophets of Baal. Elijah challenged King Ahab, Jezebel's husband, to assemble on Mount Carmel "the four hundred fifty prophets of Baal and the four hundred prophets of Asherah, who eat at Jezebel's table" (1 Kings 18:19).

Despite the odds, Elijah confidently proclaimed to all those present: "How long will you go limping with two different opinions? If the Lord is God, follow him; but if Baal, then follow him" (1 Kings 18:21). The people, however, "did not answer him a word."

Undeterred, Elijah ordered an altar to be built, after which the prophets of Baal would call upon their god to send down fire to consume a sacrificial bull. This seems to be a reasonable request to make of a god depicted with a lightning bolt in his clenched fist. We read that the prophets of Baal danced around the altar crying, "O Baal, answer us!" without success. At noon, Elijah could not resist mocking them: "Cry aloud! Surely he is a god; either he is meditating, or he has wandered away, or he is on a journey, or perhaps he is asleep and must be awakened" (1 Kings 18:27).

The earthiness of Elijah's mockery is lost in the English translation. The phrase "(perhaps) he has wandered away" in Hebrew is a euphemism for stepping aside to a private place to relieve oneself. This enraged the prophets of Baal, and they "raved on until the time of the offering of the oblation, but there was no voice, no answer, and no response" (1 Kings 18:29).

Elijah then prepared an altar, adding a trench filled with water around the altar. He offered a brief yet eloquent prayer, after which "the fire of the Lord fell and consumed the burnt offering, the wood, the stones, and the dust, and even licked up the water that was in the trench" (1 Kings 18:38).

Coincidence or Fulfilled Prophecy?

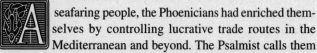 seafaring people, the Phoenicians had enriched themselves by controlling lucrative trade routes in the Mediterranean and beyond. The Psalmist calls them "the richest of the people with all kinds of wealth" (Psalm 45:12).

The Phoenicians, however, along with the other peoples of the ancient Near East, were idolaters who worshiped many gods. For hundreds of years, they also practiced infant sacrifice to appease their gods and gain their favor. Archaeologists have brought this dark side of Phoenician religion to light at their colonies at Carthage and other sites around the Mediterranean.

This practice was an abomination to the Lord, who foretold the destruction of the Phoenician city of Tyre through Ezekiel: "Therefore, thus says the Lord God: See, I am against you, O Tyre! I will hurl many nations against you, as the sea hurls its waves. They shall destroy the walls of Tyre and break down its towers. I will scrape its soil from it and make it a bare rock" (Ezekiel 26:3–4).

The reference to scraping the soil of Tyre is puzzling and occurs nowhere else in the Bible. A few verses later, another detail is added: "They will plunder your riches and loot your merchandise; they shall break down your walls and destroy your fine houses. Your stones and timber and soil they shall cast into the water" (Ezekiel 26:12).

The prophecy of Ezekiel suggests that Tyre would be utterly destroyed and that her ruins would be cast into the water. But why? While invading armies routinely destroyed cities in ancient times, they did not throw the rubble into the sea.

This prophecy appeared to make little sense—until the time of Alexander the Great. In 333 B.C., fresh from a decisive victory over the Persians in Syria, Alexander was on his way south to Egypt. He

The young warrior, Alexander the Great.

met his first opposition at Tyre. The city had been moved to a heavily defended island in the Mediterranean, some two thousand feet offshore.

Zechariah writes, the inhabitants thought they had an impregnable position: "Tyre has built itself a rampart, and heaped up silver like dust, and gold like the dirt of the streets. But now, the Lord will strip it of its possessions and hurl its wealth into the sea, and it shall be devoured by fire" (Zechariah 9:3–4).

Alexander fulfilled this prophecy when he built a causeway from the mainland to the island. He obtained the material for this massive causeway by literally scraping away the ruins of the original city on the shore.

Observing the high walls of the island fortress, Alexander's engineers designed massive movable towers that held archers and light artillery. These towers stood as high as 160 feet over the tallest defensive walls of Tyre and were the largest siege machines ever used in ancient warfare.

After seven months, the towers were completed and pushed across the causeway toward the terrified inhabitants of the city. Archers inside could quickly gain the advantage by firing down upon the hapless defenders. A drawbridge on the front enabled detachments of soldiers to climb out atop the city walls.

It was in anticipation of just such an unusual fulfillment of his prophecy that Ezekiel writes: "In their wailing they raise a lamentation for you, and lament over you: 'Who was ever destroyed like Tyre in the midst of the sea?'" (Ezekiel 27:32).

Behold the Tunnel!

Many visitors to Jerusalem are awed by the majestic walls of the old city, but they are then surprised to learn that the walls date only to 1537, when the Turkish Sultan Suleiman the Magnificent ordered them restored. Even more surprising, no doubt, is learning that the original Jerusalem stood completely outside the present walls.

The Jebusites, one of the Canaanite peoples inhabiting the land before the Israelite conquest, built the first Jerusalem as their capital. The city stood on a low ridge of land extending southward from the present-day city walls.

Though occupying only 13 acres, the city was protected by deep valleys on all sides except the north, where strong defensive fortifications made the city virtually impregnable. Hence the boast of the Jebusites to David: "You will not come in here, even the blind and the lame will turn you back"—because they thought, "David cannot come in here" (2 Samuel 5:6).

The Jebusites did not count on David's men sneaking into the city by night through the water system known as Warren's Shaft. This shaft led to the Gihon Spring, the Jebusites' water source and was the reason for their settling at the site.

The Gihon is the major natural water source in the area. A copious spring, it flows even today. In ancient times, the Gihon could supply water for a population of around 2,500.

Warren's Shaft is only one of three water systems carved out of the rock underneath the Jebusite city, today called the City of David. Solomon carved a second channel along the bottom of the hill where the city stood to provide water for irrigation of the fields in the Kidron Valley through a system of sluice gates. King Hezekiah carved out the third water system.

In Solomon's day, Israel lived securely, and besieging armies did not threaten Jerusalem. Three hundred years later, however, the situation was very different. Sennacherib and the Assyrians had already conquered the northern kingdom of Israel, and were advancing toward Jerusalem.

"When Hezekiah [king of Judah] saw that Sennacherib had come and intended to fight against Jerusalem, he planned with his officers and his warriors to stop the flow of the springs that were outside the city; and they helped him. A great many people were gathered, and they stopped all the springs and the wadi that flowed through the land, saying, 'Why should the Assyrian kings come and find water in abundance?'" (2 Chronicles 32:2–4).

Solomon's system of sluice gates may have given the impression of several springs in the Kidron Valley—here called "wadi"—but in reality they all were connected to the Gihon. The Judahites camouflaged the opening of the spring so that the Assyrians would not discover it and have access to water. This would have posed a considerable hardship upon an army, which we later read numbers more than 185,000 men.

The people of Jerusalem could not content themselves with stopping up the spring. They also needed the water. We read in 2 Chronicles how the problem was solved: "This same Hezekiah closed the upper outlet of the waters of Gihon and directed them down to the west side of the city of David" (2 Chronicles 32:30).

By the time of Hezekiah, the city limits had expanded greatly to the north and west—areas that were also protected by strong walls. The Gihon is in the Kidron Valley, which is on the east side of the City of David. By directing the water from the east to the west side, Hezekiah brought it closer to where they needed it—close to the quarter of his expanding population.

How did he bring the water across? The answer was lost until the nineteenth century, when a passage was discovered deep under the City of David. It led from the Gihon to the Pool of Siloam on the western flank of the city. Until then it was thought that the Pool of Siloam was fed by a separate spring.

The seventeen-hundred-foot-long water channel was known as Hezekiah's Tunnel. It is an admirable feat of engineering made even more remarkable by the discovery of an ancient inscription written by its excavators. This eighth-century B.C. inscription, now in the Istanbul museum, reads in part: "Behold the tunnel. This is the story of its cutting. While the miners swung their picks, one towards the other, and when there remained only 3 cubits to cut, the voice of one calling to his fellow was heard.... So the day they broke through the miners struck, one against the other, pick against pick, and the water flowed from the spring towards the pool, 1200 cubits. The height of the rock above the head of the miners was 100 cubits."

One puzzle remained, however. The tunnel is not carved in a straight path to the Pool of Siloam. It takes a serpentine, round-about route, which adds hundreds of feet to its length. Since they dug the tunnel in haste as the Assyrians advanced toward Jerusalem, it seems odd that the engineers would intentionally complicate what was already a daunting task.

Some have suggested that the excavators miscalculated, resulting in a crooked tunnel, but this is not likely. Engineers in ancient times were fully capable of excavating straight channels, as can be seen in the water tunnel at Megiddo.

The inscription found in the tunnel shows that Hezekiah's engineers knew what they were doing. They correctly calculated both the distance and the depth of the tunnel underground.

Recent examination of the tunnel provides the likely reason for Hezekiah's crooked tunnel. The evidence shows that the path of the tunnel followed a natural fissure in the rock that wound its way circuitously underneath the City of David. Rather than carve a completely new channel through the hard limestone, the engineers decided to follow and enlarge an existing crevice.

What seems at first glance to have been much more work, was actually easier than attempting to carve a direct route—an important consideration considering the approaching menace of the Assyrian army.

Passing Through the Fire

he Topheth lies in the valley of Hinnom. As the kingdom of Judah (the southern territory of the Israelites) fell into moral degradation, the Judahites sacrificed their sons and daughters at the Topheth. There are only a few scattered references to the Topheth in the Bible.

The worship of Baal, the preeminent Canaanite deity, is mentioned in relation to the Topheth, as is the Ammonite god Molech. The Bible describes the ominous-sounding practice of "building the high place of Topheth, which is in the valley of the son of Hinnom, to burn their sons and their daughters in the fire" (Jeremiah 7:31).

Exactly what "burning in the fire" meant eluded biblical scholars until the discovery of similar sites, also called "Topheths," at

Phoenician Carthage, Sicily, Sardinia, and Tunisia. The Topheth found at Carthage is the largest known cemetery of sacrificed humans from the ancient world. For more than six hundred years, child sacrifice was performed at the site, which is believed to contain tens of thousands of urns filled with the remains of children.

In the third century B.C., Greek writer Kleitarchos described child sacrifice at Carthage. He said that whenever the Carthaginians desired to obtain something of special importance, they would vow one of their children to Kronos, the Greek equivalent to the Phoenician god Baal-Hammon. The Topheth was dedicated to Baal-Hammon's consort Tanit, who was the chief goddess of the Phoenicians.

But it is Kleitarchos' account of how the sacrifices were performed that may provide the key for understanding what the biblical phrase "passing through the fire" meant. In the middle of the Topheth at Carthage stood a bronze statue of Kronos, its open hands extended over a heated bronze brazier. The victim was placed into the fiery hands of the god Kronos and was consumed by the flames from the brazier.

Even the Romans, who tolerated infanticide as a form of birth control, found the child sacrifices at Carthage to be despicable. The Roman theologian Tertullian describes how the emperor Tiberius hanged the priests who conducted the sacrifices from the very trees of the Topheth.

It may be that similar depravities performed in the Topheth in the valley of Hinnom only came to an end once and for all with the destruction of Jerusalem in 586 B.C.

There Is a Balm in Gilead

n his deep longing for the spiritual renewal of his fellow Judeans, the prophet Jeremiah laments: "Is there no balm in Gilead? Is there no physician there? Why then has the health of my poor people not been restored?" (Jeremiah 8:22).

In the ancient Near East, aromatic resins or gums, known as balms, were widely used for medicinal and cosmetic purposes. According to tradition, the balm of Gilead was also used to anoint the kings of Israel.

The fact that several different "balms" are referred to in the Bible complicates accurate identification of the balm of Gilead. However, the Talmud, the exhaustive Jewish interpretation of the Hebrew Bible, identifies the balm of Gilead with balsam. Near-miraculous properties are ascribed to this oil, which is credited with everything from healing wounds to making men wild with lust.

The first-century Jewish historian Josephus states that balsam trees were first brought to Israel and presented as a gift to King Solomon by the Queen of Sheba. The Book of 1 Kings confirms that the Queen of Sheba presented to Solomon "a great quantity of spices, and precious stones; never again did spices come in such quantity as that which the queen of Sheba gave to King Solomon" (1 Kings 10:10).

According to ancient sources in the Near East, balsam was only grown at locations near the Dead Sea: Jericho, Zoar, and En-Gedi.

So renowned was the balm of Gilead from En-Gedi that, after suppressing the First Judean Revolt, the Roman commander Titus displayed balsam branches in his victory march through Rome.

Excavation at the oasis of En-Gedi reveals a long history of Jewish occupation, despite extreme conditions and scant rainfall, which make farming difficult. How, then, did En-Gedi survive? The answer is found in the profitable cultivation of the thorny, shrublike balsam tree. The economy of En-Gedi was centered around it. Archaeologists have uncovered ovens used to process the tree's valuable oil, and the large barrel-shaped pottery jars used to store it.

It was at En-Gedi that archaeologists uncovered a baffling curse in an inscription on a synagogue floor: "Whoever reveals the secret of the village to the gentiles, the one whose eyes roam over the entire earth and see what is concealed will uproot this person and his seed from under the sun."

Archaeologists puzzled over the curse for more than 25 years until subsequent excavations revealed a possible answer. In a large tower thought to be used to produce balsam, large vats were discovered. The design of the vats suggested that they contained not water but oil, leading archaeologists to conclude that the balsam was processed by boiling it in oil.

Could it have been this "secret recipe" for processing balsam that was a jealously guarded secret of the En-Gedi community? The curse in the synagogue floor may have been intended to ensure that En-Gedi continued to corner the market on the balm of Gilead.

The Search for the Lost Ark

aiders of the Lost Ark, Steven Spielberg's hugely successful movie, popularized what some consider a serious endeavor—searching for the biblical Ark of the Covenant. Interestingly, other, more popular views have superseded the premise of the movie—the Ark was taken by Pharaoh Shishak of Egypt in the tenth century B.C.

According to Jewish tradition (as recorded in the Book of 2 Maccabees), at the time of the fall of Jerusalem in 586 B.C., the prophet Jeremiah "ordered that the tent and the Ark should follow with him, and he went out to the mountain where Moses had gone up and he had seen the inheritance of God. Jeremiah came and found a cave-dwelling, and he brought there the tent and the ark and the altar of incense; and he sealed up the entrance" (2 Maccabees 2:4–5).

Moses died on Mount Nebo in Transjordan. When some of his followers attempted to mark the location on the mountain, Jeremiah rebuked them, saying: "The place shall remain unknown until God gathers his people together again and shows his mercy" (2 Maccabees 2:7). Some investigators, convinced they were living in the time when the location of the Ark would be revealed, scoured Mount Nebo in hopes of finding it. However, with only one discredited claim of the Ark having been found under an ancient church on nearby Mount Pisgah, there is no evidence of the Ark's presence on the mountain.

Others believe the Ark was hidden near the ancient Essene settlement of Qumran by the Dead Sea. However, the excavation of numerous caves has proved fruitless in the search for the Ark. Still others theorize that the Ark remained closer to home and suggest a number of sites in Jerusalem, including a tunnel under the city and at Gordon's Calvary, the possible site of the crucifixion of Christ.

Many ultraorthodox Jews believe the Ark is hidden in a secret chamber carved deep under the Temple Mount, waiting to be revealed when the Temple is rebuilt. It is thought that the builder of the first temple, King Solomon, foresaw a time when the Ark would need to be hidden, and he carved out an underground chamber.

Where might the Ark of the Covenant rest?

Don't confuse this subterranean chamber with the cave under the bedrock inside the Dome of the Rock. Any tourist may enter that today. In the early 1980s, archaeologists were excavating underground along the western retaining wall of the so-called Second Temple, built by King Herod. The Second Temple, built on the same location, was a much larger and grander edifice than Solomon's original Temple.

Orthodox rabbis were building a synagogue adjoining the wall when they accidentally broke through an ancient subterranean gate that led into the temple. Entering through a hole in

the wall, they discovered a hall approximately 75 feet long leading in the direction of the area thought to be the Holy of Holies.
The tunnel, however, was filled with mud and water, which the
rabbis and their workers drained and cleaned out.

They proceeded with their clandestine excavation cautiously,
fearing that the Muslims controlling the Temple Mount above
them would discover the project and demand an end to their digging. After 18 months of these secret excavations, the passage-
way ended at a sealed wall. The rabbis were convinced that
somewhere on the other side lay the Holy of Holies and the Ark
of the Covenant.

At this point, Muslim authorities learned of the excavation.
A riot was narrowly averted, and the Israeli government forced
the rabbis to end their excavations and seal up the tunnel.

The rabbis remain convinced that the Ark of the Covenant
lies somewhere deep beneath the Temple Mount and that it will
be brought to light one day when, as 2 Maccabees states, "God
gathers his people together again and shows his mercy."

Is the Ark in Ethiopia?

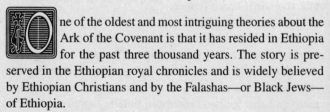 ne of the oldest and most intriguing theories about the
Ark of the Covenant is that it has resided in Ethiopia
for the past three thousand years. The story is preserved in the Ethiopian royal chronicles and is widely believed
by Ethiopian Christians and by the Falashas—or Black Jews—
of Ethiopia.

According to the chronicles, the Queen of Sheba mentioned in the Bible was from Ethiopia. She had a son named Menelik I by King Solomon. The Ark is said to have been secretly taken from Jerusalem by Menelik, with the assistance of the priests, after Solomon's death.

The Ark is reportedly kept in Saint Mary of Zion Church in Axum, Ethiopia, and can only be viewed once a year when they bring it out for a special ceremony. However, scholars think the covered object paraded during the ceremony is a replica of the true Ark.

The theory that the Ark of the Covenant is in Ethiopia has serious difficulties. For one, scholars believe that the kingdom of the Queen of Sheba was in the area of southwest Arabia known as the land of Yemen, not in Africa. Also, it is doubtful whether anyone could have succeeded in removing the Ark from the Holy of Holies. Entering the Holy of Holies is almost inconceivable for anyone—even priests; only the High Priest was permitted to enter it, and only on one day each year.

It does not, in any case, appear that the Ark was moved at such an early date as the Ethiopian theory requires. There is a reference to the Ark during the time of Josiah, almost 300 years after the time when it was thought to have been taken to Ethiopia: "[Josiah] said to the Levites who taught all Israel and were holy to the Lord, 'Put the holy ark in the house that Solomon son of David, king of Israel, built; you need no longer carry it on your shoulders" (2 Chronicles 35:3).

It appears that the Ark was still in Jerusalem at a much later time than allowed by those who believe the Ethiopian theory.

An Ancient Fingerprint

We read in the Book of Jeremiah that a scribe named Baruch assisted the prophet: "Then Jeremiah called Baruch son of Neriah, and Baruch wrote on a scroll at Jeremiah's dictation all the words of the Lord that he had spoken to him" (Jeremiah 36:4). It is this very same Baruch who has the distinction of being the only ancient personage whose fingerprint is thought to be known.

In a remarkable correlation with the biblical text, the name "Baruch" appears on an ancient seal known as a "bulla" unearthed at the City of David excavations in Jerusalem. The bulla, a lump of clay impressed with a seal, was used to secure documents, which in Jeremiah's day were scrolls. They would tie with string and then seal the scroll with the lump of clay to identify the owner.

The bulla found at the City of David is dated to the late seventh or sixth century B.C., the last years of the kingdom of Judah chronicled by the prophet Jeremiah. It reads: "Belonging to Berekhyahu, son of Neriyahu, the Scribe." Berekhyahu is the long form of the name Baruch, meaning "Blessed of Yahweh." The identification of this seal with the biblical Baruch is confirmed by the fact that Baruch's father is called Neriah—a variant of Neriyahu—in the Bible.

The location where the seal was found also fits with what we know of Jeremiah. The seal was found near what is known as the "stepped-stone structure" thought to be a retaining wall for David's palace in ancient Jerusalem. Jeremiah frequently appeared before the king of Jerusalem and would have been present in the same place where archaeologists uncovered the seal.

Another bulla bearing the same name was found, this one contained a fingerprint on the edge. Since Baruch would have been the person to use this seal containing his name, there is little doubt that it is the fingerprint of the biblical personage Baruch.

In the Book of Jeremiah, the prophet states: "And I gave the deed of purchase to Baruch son of Neriah son of Mahseiah, in the presence of my cousin Hanamel, in the presence of the witnesses who signed the deed of purchase, and in the presence of all the Judeans who were sitting in the court of the guard" (Jeremiah 32:12).

It was during the signing and sealing of this document, or another like it, that the fingerprint of Baruch was preserved for all time.

The Fall of Babylon

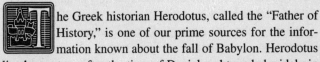 he Greek historian Herodotus, called the "Father of History," is one of our prime sources for the information known about the fall of Babylon. Herodotus lived a century after the time of Daniel and traveled widely in the East.

In his *Histories,* we learn of the campaign of Persia's King Cyrus against Babylon. Herodotus provides many illuminating details, including the fact that no Persian king, including Cyrus, would drink the water of any stream other than the Choaspes, a river that flows past the Persian capital of Susa. Wherever the king went, a long train of four-wheeled mule wagons followed him transporting silver jars filled with the river's water—which, curiously, was always boiled.

On his march to Babylon, Cyrus was preparing to cross the Gyndes River when one of his sacred white horses fell into

the swift current and was carried away. Furious that the river would dare take one of his prized steeds, he vowed to make it so tame that a woman could cross it without getting her knees wet. Temporarily forsaking his march on

Babylon fell to the Persians.

Babylon, he marked off 180 channels to be dug on either side of the river. The diverted water reduced the flow of the Gyndes to little more than a trickle.

Having taken his revenge, Cyrus resumed his march on Babylon, where the defenders of the great city were waiting for him. After attacking Cyrus' troops unsuccessfully, they retreated within the massive city walls. Herodotus writes that the Babylonians were well prepared for a long siege, having accumulated enough food to last for years.

The siege of the city seemed to accomplish little, and Cyrus was beginning to despair when he remembered his experience with the Gyndes, setting a brilliant strategy in motion. The seemingly impenetrable walls of Babylon had one weak point, where the Euphrates River flowed under them on its course directly through the middle of Babylon. Cyrus stationed his troops near where the river entered and exited the city. He then went upstream with his construction troops to a point where it was possible to divert the river. His men worked furiously, careful not to give themselves away, and soon the depth of the river was reduced to no more than the middle of a man's thigh. Cyrus' troops waited until nightfall and swept into the city.

Herodotus reports that, if they had been aware of Cyrus' strategy, the Babylonians could have attacked the invading troops from the walls overlooking the river. Another reason for Cyrus' success was that the people of the city were celebrating the feast of Belshazzar, dancing and enjoying themselves while the Persians entered Babylon by stealth.

A Fateful Night in Babylon

 t is a story almost too fantastic to be true, or so many scholars thought, but new evidence is shedding light on the last evening in the life of King Belshazzar and his kingdom.

We read in the Book of Daniel that Belshazzar made a great feast for a thousand of his lords. As the wine flowed, the king was in a boastful mood, and he ordered that the gold and silver vessels that his father, Nebuchadnezzar, had taken from the Temple of Jerusalem be brought out so that his guests could drink from them.

To use the sacred objects for drunken revelry was more than a show of contempt. To those present, the act would be yet another reminder of the humiliation that the Jews suffered in the conquest of their country and the carrying off of their temple treasures.

What happened next put an instant end to the festivities. As the glasses were filled and the gods of Babylon were praised, suddenly the hall fell silent. A finger appeared and began to write on the wall. No one present understood the meaning of the four words: *MENE, MENE, TEKEL, PARSIN*.

The text then describes Belshazzar's response: "The king was watching the hand as it wrote. Then the king's face turned pale, and his thoughts terrified him. His limbs gave way, and his knees knocked together" (Daniel 5:5–6). He immediately called for his magicians and diviners, promising the third place in his kingdom for whoever succeeded in interpreting the writing.

The wise men of Babylon, however, were unable to translate the writing. Then the queen suggested that Belshazzar summon Daniel, the prophet of Judah who had interpreted the visions of Nebuchadnezzar years earlier. Hastened to the banquet hall, Daniel told Belshazzar the meaning of the strange words.

The message was one of doom: "MENE, God has numbered the days of your kingdom and brought it to an end; TEKEL, you have been weighed on the scales and found wanting; PERES [the singular of Parsin], your kingdom is divided and given to the Medes and Persians" (Daniel 5:26–28). According to the text, Belshazzar was killed that very night as the Medes and the Persians conquered the kingdom of Babylon.

The traditional setting for this story as told in the Book of Daniel is sixth-century B.C. Babylon. In the third century A.D., Porphyry, a philosopher and opponent of Christianity, challenged the sixth-century date for the book. Porphyry dated the Book of Daniel to 165 B.C., arguing that it foretold events so accurately that it must have been written after the events occurred.

With the rise of biblical criticism in the last century, this view became widely accepted among scholars, who viewed the Book of Daniel as a second-century B.C. Jewish national folktale containing little of historical value. The fact that, until the mid-nineteenth century, Belshazzar's name was nowhere to be found outside the biblical text lent support to the later date. Nebuchadnezzar was included in the ancient lists of Babylonian kings preserved by the Greeks. But the name of the last native ruler of Babylon and successor to Nebuchadnezzar was listed as Nabonidus, not Belshazzar.

Then, in 1854, several small clay cylinders were uncovered in the temple of the moon god in Babylon. Only four inches long, each cylinder was inscribed with 60 or so lines of the wedge-shaped cuneiform writing used in ancient Mesopotamia. When deciphered, they were found to be a prayer for good health and a long life for Nabonidus, who ruled Babylon from 555 to 539 B.C. The prayer also included mention of his eldest son, identified on the cylinder as Belshazzar.

There was no longer any doubt that Belshazzar existed, but he was identified in the cylinder only as the king's son. The mystery deepened as several other references to Belshazzar were discovered in the following decades, and in every case he is identified as the king's son or as the crown prince, never as king.

And yet there was still something amiss. Legal documents from the sixth-century B.C.

Belshazzar sees the writing on the wall.

uniformly include an oath only to the god and the king. The documents swearing by Nabonidus and his son Belshazzar were the only known exceptions to this standard practice. This implied a unique relationship between Nabonidus and Belshazzar.

Other evidence became known regarding the two men from ancient Babylonia. It seems that Nabonidus was an eccentric ruler who spurned the usual gods of Babylon in favor of Harran and the moon god Ur. Significantly, for several years Nabonidus abandoned Babylon and resided at the distant oasis of Teima in northern Arabia. It was during Nabonidus' absence from the throne that Belshazzar ruled in his stead.

The word for king in Aramaic, the language of much of the Book of Daniel, is a broad term that can mean "governor" or "crown prince." This is precisely how Belshazzar functioned as the regent of Nabonidus.

This solution solves another puzzle in the story. We read that Belshazzar promised that whoever could read the writing on the wall would "rank third in the kingdom" (Daniel 5:7). Why would that person be third in the kingdom instead of second—as, for example, had been granted Joseph by Pharaoh (Genesis 41:40, 44)? The answer, it appears, is that Belshazzar was already the second ruler, after Nabonidus. The highest position that could be offered Daniel was that of third ruler over the kingdom.

It seems, then, that the story of Daniel fits well into the setting of Babylon in the sixth century B.C. There is no evidence outside the Bible for the writing on the wall, nor could any be reasonably expected.

We do, however, have one last confirmation of the events of the Book of Daniel in the testimony of Greek historian Herodotus. Writing a century after the fall of Babylon, Herodotus confirmed that a festival was in progress at the very hour that the Persians entered the city.

The Handwriting on the Wall

 t his fateful last feast, King Belshazzar called for the sages, enchanters, and diviners of Babylon to interpret the four words that mysteriously appeared on the wall of the banquet hall. He did so with every expectation that they would be able to decipher the message, for throughout its history, Babylon was renowned for explaining the hidden messages of omens.

Archaeologists have uncovered several ancient libraries containing large numbers of cuneiform tablets dealing with the subject of omens and how to interpret them. In ancient Babylon, enormous effort was devoted to collecting and archiving the meaning of cryptic signs. Dreams, extraordinary circumstances, the unusual behavior of animals, patterns in the sky, or in smoke, or in oil on water—all were considered omens of some future event, be it good or evil.

It was considered vital that the omens be properly interpreted so that danger could be averted. If, for example, what was taken to be a sign appeared before a defeat in battle, whenever the same sign occurred before military conflict, it would be taken as a warning to avoid battle until a more favorable time.

Over time, literally thousands of signs and their supposed meanings were catalogued by the diviners of Babylon. But on the night of the fall of Babylon, when Belshazzar commanded his wise men to interpret the writing on the wall, the lists proved worthless. Nothing like this had ever happened before.

The message that appeared on the wall—MENE, MENE, TEKEL, PARSIN—was Aramaic, a language well known both to the wise men and to Daniel. The first, Mene, is a unit of weight: 50 shekels or about 1¼ pounds: The second, Tekel, is the Aramaic word for shekel, the basic unit of monetary value. Parsin is a fraction of a shekel.

Read literally, the words had no meaning, and the diviners were unable to decipher them. Daniel, however, was able to beat the Babylonian magicians at their own game. The root meaning of Mene is "to count"; similarly, Tekel can mean "to weigh." For the last word, Daniel determined that a play on the sound of the word was intended; Parsin is closely related to the Aramaic word for "Persian." The meaning, then, was that Babylon was weighed and found wanting. The similarity of Parsin to "Persian" left little doubt as to the meaning of the message: Babylon would fall to the Persians.

This interpretation somehow escaped the sages, even though the city was at that moment under siege by the Persians.

Daniel might well have said to Belshazzar what he told King Nebuchadnezzar before him: "No wise men, enchanters, magicians, or diviners can show to the king the mystery that the king is asking, but there is a God in heaven who reveals mysteries" (Daniel 2:27).

Countdown to Gog and Magog

he Book of Ezekiel indicates that the battle of Gog and Magog will take place after a great worldwide dispersion of the Jews, known as the Diaspora. The Jews are destined to return to their own land: "But you, O mountains of Israel, shall shoot out your branches, and yield your fruit to my people Israel; for they shall soon come home" (Ezekiel 36:8).

Historically, there have been only two possibilities for this prophesied return. The first is in the second century B.C., when

Judea was controlled by the successors to the Greeks, known as the Seleucids. In 169 B.C., the Jews, horrified when Antiochus IV desecrated their Temple with a pagan altar, revolted.

The Maccabean brothers led the charge against the Seleucids, whose weaponry included a herd of 32 elephants. With God on their side, the Maccabees were convinced that the powers of evil—which they equated with their Seleucid overlords—would be vanquished.

The Jews fought brilliantly, eventually triumphing over their foes and establishing the Hasmonean kingdom. Many of them undoubtedly thought the independent Jewish kingdom they had established was the fulfillment of Ezekiel's prophecy. Their messianic expectations would eventually fade, however, as the Hasmonean dynasty became torn with internal dissent. Rome intervened in 63 B.C., putting an end to the Jewish nation.

The second historical possibility for the return of the Jews to their homeland occurred in modern times. In 1948, after nineteen hundred years of Diaspora, the Jewish people once again established an independent Jewish state in the land of Israel, despite fierce opposition from Arab neighbors.

Many believe the modern state of Israel is the fulfillment of the ancient prophecy of Ezekiel, which speaks of a restored nation "where people were gathered from many nations on the mountains of Israel, which had long lain waste; its people were brought out from the nations and now are living in safety, all of them" (Ezekiel 38:8).

Whereas, during the Hasmonean period, the Jews returned from one nation (Babylon), the modern state of Israel is composed of Jews from more than a hundred nations, thus fulfilling the prophesy that "many nations" would return. Ezekiel also states that the Jews would return to a land "which had long lain waste," a fitting description of the land of Palestine until the influx of immigrants who planted fields and orchards and built modern cities in the nineteenth and twentieth centuries.

Finally, the reference to the people of Israel "living in safety" may refer to the safety that comes from military security. If so, then it is a fitting parallel to modern Israel. Few nations invest as much in their military as the Jewish nation, which requires all young men and women to serve in the army and which has repeatedly demonstrated its capabilities on the battlefield.

And yet, when all the evidence is presented, it still doesn't add up to absolute certainty. It is entirely possible that political changes or future military conflict in the unstable Middle East will change the geopolitical map into something quite different from the way it appears today.

It is also a very real possibility that the identification of the modern state of Israel with the return mentioned in Ezekiel is mistaken. More than two thousand years ago, the Hasmoneans believed they had good reason to think that they were the fulfillment of Ezekiel's prophecy.

Consider also that the Hasmonean kingdom, which lasted more than a hundred years, was larger and more "religious" than modern Israel. The supreme Jewish council, known as the San-hedrin, was in session then, and daily sacrifices were being offered in the Temple, none of which is taking place today in modern Israel.

All of which goes to show that interpreting biblical prophecy requires both a thorough knowledge of the past and a cautious approach to the future.

Esther: Folklore or History?

he Book of Esther tells the story of a beautiful young Hebrew woman who thwarts a massacre of the Israelites in Persia during the fifth century B.C. It is a favorite among Jews and is the biblical basis for the holiday of Purim.

Rabbis hesitated to include the Book of Esther in the Hebrew canon because it is the only book in the Bible where the name of God is found. It is also the only biblical book not found among the treasure trove of documents discovered at Qumran near the shores of the Dead Sea.

The value of the book, however, eventually convinced skeptics, and Esther was included in the canon. It is an exceptional tale that beautifully characterizes virtue in the persons of Esther and Mordecai, at the same time portraying the ultimate in homicidal arrogance in the archvillain Haman.

In fact, the book is so well plotted and entertaining to read that critics consider it little more than a Jewish folktale. However, from archaeological and historical sources, it now seems evident that the Book of Esther is soundly rooted in history.

The story begins with a lavish banquet in the palace of Xerxes (called Ahasuerus in Esther), king of Persia. Queen Vashti is ordered to make an appearance and display her beauty to the assembled participants. She refuses and consequently is deposed. The search begins for a new queen, and after a full year of beauty treatments—apparently standard procedure for Persian harems—Esther is chosen to succeed Vashti.

The story takes an ominous turn when Esther's Uncle Mordecai, who sits at the gate of the city, learns that two of the royal bodyguards are plotting to assassinate the king. He informs Esther and the plot is foiled.

Enter Haman the Agagite, a high official of Xerxes who becomes enraged when Mordecai does not bow down to him when he passes by.

Queen Esther faints before her king.

Learning that Mordecai is a Jew, he convinces King Xerxes that Jews are a disobedient people who should not be tolerated. Xerxes issues a proclamation that allows the murder and plunder of the Jews of Persia.

Mordecai persuades Esther to use her influence with the king to have the proclamation canceled. Esther gathers her courage to make her request, knowing full well the stakes: Under penalty of death, no one is allowed to enter the presence of the king uninvited.

Esther is successful, and the decree against the Jews is ultimately rescinded. Haman is humiliated by being commanded to walk through the city, leading the royal steed on which his adversary Mordecai, one of the Jews he wanted killed, is seated—an honor Haman thought was being reserved for himself.

It is a captivating story, wryly written and full of both the pitfalls of human nature and the triumph of forthrightness. But it is more than that. Details of the story reflect intimate familiarity with Persian life and culture of the fifth century B.C.

Some of the evidence is linguistic. Old Persian terms used in the book went out of use during the fourth century B.C. This indicates that the book was written during the actual time when the events took place.

As for Mordecai, historical sources indicate at least one similar name, Marduka, who was a scribe at Susa. Foreigners served in the Persian court, as did Nehemiah, who had the honored position of cupbearer to the king (Nehemiah 2:1).

The Book of Esther describes Mordecai as sitting at the king's gate. In ancient Persia, the entrance to the palace was an important administrative center for the royal court. The Hebrew word for "sit" may actually mean to occupy an official position, perhaps akin to serving in the palace guard. Mordecai's presence at the gate was likely a sign of his importance.

King Xerxes' lavish banquet described at the beginning of the Book of Esther was held in "the third year of his reign." Historical sources record that during his first two years on the throne, Xerxes was occupied with rebellions in Egypt and Babylonia.

After Vashti's refusal at the banquet, we read that Xerxes consulted "the seven officials of Persia and Media, who had access to the king, and sat first in the kingdom" (Esther 1:14). The existence of this council, which served the Persian king, is confirmed by Greek sources.

There is one more historical detail that lends credence to the story of Esther. At the end of the book, we read that King Xerxes "laid tribute on the land and on the islands of the sea" (Esther 10:1). The only islands that the Persians are known to have controlled were in the Aegean Sea. In 480–479 B.C., the Persians fought unsuccessfully to retain control of these islands.

Thus, the date for the setting of Esther in the third year of Xerxes' reign (482 B.C.) fits well within the historical context, and the Book of Esther remains a glorious account of triumph over the specter of persecution.

What Motivated Cyrus?

yrus the Great, King of Persia, overthrew the Babylonian empire in 539 B.C., an event that would bring about the return of the Jews to their homeland.

Shortly after ascending the throne, King Cyrus declared: "The Lord, the God of heaven, has given me all the kingdoms of the earth, and he has charged me to build him a house at Jerusalem in Judah. Any of those among you who are of his people—may their God be with them!—are now permitted to go up to Jerusalem in Judah . . ." (Ezra 1:1–3).

The remains of Babylon.

How did the Lord stir up the spirit of Cyrus to permit the Jews to return to Jerusalem? Some have suggested that Cyrus was aware of the prophecies of Isaiah, which foretold the return of the Jews and mention Cyrus by name: "Thus says the Lord . . . who says of Cyrus, 'He is my shepherd, and he shall carry out all my purpose'; and who says of Jerusalem, 'It shall be rebuilt,' and of the temple, 'Your foundation shall be laid'" (Isaiah 44:28).

Precisely because of the references to Cyrus, many scholars reject the traditional dating of the writings of Isaiah to the eighth century B.C. in favor of a sixth-century date for at least the second half of the book (Isaiah 40–66). It is not possible, they point out, for Isaiah to have known of Cyrus more than 50 years before he was born. Therefore, the Book of Isaiah must have been written after the time of Cyrus.

However, the dating of the Book of Isaiah to the eighth century is supported by the ancient Jewish historian Josephus, who insisted that Cyrus did indeed know of the prophecies of Isaiah and of his foretold role in enabling the Jews to return to their land. Author of *The History of the Jews,* Josephus was intimately acquainted with the history of his people and had access to many source materials now lost. Josephus believed that the Book of Isaiah must have been written before Cyrus' time in order for him to have read it.

The prophet Daniel was still living during the early years of Cyrus' reign. His esteemed position would have made him a likely candidate to introduce Cyrus to the prophecies of Isaiah, particularly those regarding him. There is every reason to suspect that seeing his name in the ancient Jewish prophecies would have profoundly affected the Persian monarch, perhaps even enough to let the Israelites go.

A discovery made during the excavation of Babylon confirms the biblical account of Cyrus' freeing of captive peoples. The "Cyrus cylinder," a ten-inch-long barrel-shaped cylinder made of clay, details the royal policy regarding captives: "[Cyrus] gathered all their [former] inhabitants and returned [to them] their inhabitations." Here we do have a nonbiblical reference to the "spirit" of Cyrus.

Darius: Not Just a Face on a Coin

After Cyrus the Great decreed that the Jews should be allowed to rebuild their temple, their foes succeeded in delaying the project for decades. According to the Book of Ezra, the inhabitants of neighboring lands "bribed officials to frustrate their plan throughout the reign of King Cyrus

Relief of King Darius.

of Persia and until the reign of King Darius of Persia" (Ezra 4:5).

With the ascension of Darius to the throne, work on the temple finally began, but not before the opponents of the Jews appealed to the Persian ruler. Ezra contains several fascinating letters between the various parties and the Persian monarch. Darius had an extensive search made of the royal archives and found the original decree of Cyrus, which permitted the rebuilding, thus settling the issue.

What do we know about this ruler who figures so prominently—if only in the background—of the rebuilding of the Jewish temple? Fortunately, quite a lot. The Persians were skilled at chronicling their history, even though it invariably presented their rulers in a positive light.

Darius, who reigned from 522 to 486 B.C., was the second in a line of succession after Cyrus the Great and his successor Cambyses. His rule of nearly 40 years breathed new life into the Persian empire, which had been fragmented by revolt prior to his ascension.

This upheaval in the empire may be that which is referred to in the Book of Haggai, written during the time of the rebuilding of the temple. "For thus says the Lord of hosts: Once again, in a little while, I will shake the heavens and the earth and the sea and the dry land; and I will shake all the nations, so that the treasure of all nations shall come, and I will fill this house with splendor, says the Lord of hosts" (Haggai 2:6–7).

The correspondence between Darius and various parties preserved in the Book of Ezra indicates an efficient administration of the empire, a fact confirmed by history. Darius divided his empire into 20 provinces. He built major roads and established a uniform standard of weights and measures. He has also been credited with issuing the world's first currency. A gold coin known as the Daric was stamped with Darius' own likeness, showing him running and holding a spear and bow.

The Persian ruler carefully examined the contention between the Judeans and their opponents, and he paid deference to the decrees of his predecessors. This indicates an empire that observed at least some semblance of a legal system.

Despite his considerable achievements, Darius also presided over one of the worst defeats of the Persian empire, at the hands of the Greeks, at the Battle of Marathon in 490 B.C. The battle marked a turning point in Persian history, after which the empire entered a period of permanent decline.

<u>SOME BACKGROUND</u>
Josephus: The Amazing Adventurer and Scholar

xcept for the New Testament, our primary source of knowledge about first-century Judea is the Jewish historian, Josephus. If we believe what he writes about himself, his life was full of fascinating exploits and adventures.

In A.D. 37, Josephus was born into a well-established priestly family in Jerusalem. Educated in a rabbinical school, he became an authority on the law by the time he was 14. At 16 he was studying the major Jewish religious parties—the Pharisees, Sadducees, and Essenes—to decide which to join.

Josephus then spent three years in the desert meditating with a hermit. When he returned at age 19, Josephus had become a Pharisee. Seven years of priestly duties passed uneventfully, but at age 26 he went to Rome on a minor diplomatic mission and was shipwrecked on the way.

In A.D. 66, Judea was on the eve of revolt against Rome. Josephus—a priest and scholar—was hardly qualified for military leadership. But through a series of unusual circumstances, he was appointed commander of Galilee.

Josephus rose to the occasion, leading his men bravely in defense of their fortress at Jotapata. After a two-month siege, Jotapata was about to fall. Josephus and the last of his men hid out in a cave, where they decided to commit mass suicide rather than surrender to the Romans.

Josephus suggested they draw lots, and one by one his men submitted to having their throats slit until only he and one other man were left. This remarkable coincidence, Josephus later said was due either to luck or divine providence.

Josephus convinced his fellow survivor that surrendering would be better after all. They were brought before Vespasian, commander of the Roman legion. Again he managed to save himself. He surprised Vespasian by playing the seer and prophesying that Vespasian was destined to become emperor of Rome.

Curious about this prophet, Vespasian kept him at his headquarters for the next two years, at which time Nero was dethroned and Vespasian proclaimed emperor. Josephus remained in the entourage of Vespasian's son Titus, who completed the conquest of Judea. His presence

Engraving of Jewish historian Josephus.

during Jerusalem's destruction was the basis for his riveting eye-witness account of the siege.

Scholars debate the accuracy of Josephus' account of his exploits during the Jewish revolt. It is likely that some of what he wrote was intended to justify his own conduct in deserting to the Romans, while tactfully avoiding offending his captors.

After the war, Titus granted Josephus an estate outside Jerusalem in reward for his services. However, having angered his fellow Jews because of his dealings with Rome, he wisely decided to leave the country. In Rome, Josephus was granted citizenship and a lifetime pension, and he was given Vespasian's private home to live in. It is here that he spent the rest of his life recording the history of his homeland, Judea.

In gratitude for the privileges bestowed upon him, Josephus took the family name of the ruling Flavius dynasty as his own, and so Joseph of Matthias became Flavius Josephus.

How Many Herods Can You Count?

tudents of the Bible are sometimes confused by the various rulers named Herod mentioned in the New Testament. The name "Herod" became a title assumed by his descendants, much like the Roman emperors after Julius Caesar were called "Caesar."

The family tree of Herod the Great was more sparse than it would have been had he not murdered so many of his own family. Among his victims were his Hasmonean wife Miriam, their two sons Alexander and Aristobulus, and a son by another of his wives named Antipater.

After Herod died, his three surviving sons (Archelaus, Antipas, and Philip) fought for control over his domain. Augustus Caesar intervened, resolving the dispute by dividing the kingdom into three parts. Archelaus was given Judea, Samaria, and Idumea, along with the lesser title of "ethnarch."

The Herodians

We read in the Gospel of Matthew that, along with the Pharisees, representatives from a party called the Herodians came to Jesus and said to him: "Teacher, we know that you are sincere, and show deference to no one; for you do not regard people with partiality, but teach the way of God in accordance with truth. Is it lawful to pay taxes to the emperor, or not?" (Mark 12:14).

The question the Herodians asked revealed their basic sympathies: As their name suggests, they were supporters of Herod Antipas, who ruled in Judea after the death of his father, Herod the Great. The Herodians lent enthusiastic support to Herod to a much greater degree than the Pharisees and the Sadducees, but we are not certain why. The Herodians may have been a small group with close, perhaps familial, ties to their rulers.

In asking the question, they wanted to trip up Jesus in front of one or another of the sects and parties of first-century Judea.

As a bonus, Antipas would have been keenly interested in hearing about anyone advocating "tax revolt" in his kingdom. If Jesus' answer had supported such a revolt, one can assume that the Herodians would have wasted no time reporting him to Antipas.

The Zealots, a sect with considerable popular sympathy, abhorred the idea of paying taxes to Rome. If, on the other hand, Jesus' words could be understood as lending support to the ruling powers, he would likely have alienated the populace.

"Give to Caesar what is Caesar's, and to God what is God's." His answer was brilliant, silencing both sides, and bearing testimony to the divine inspiration that guided Jesus.

On another occasion, after he silenced those who opposed his ministry, we read: "The Pharisees went out and immediately conspired with the Herodians against him, how to destroy him" (Mark 3:6). So began the plotting that would eventually culminate in Jesus' crucifixion.

It was fear of Archelaus that caused Joseph to take Mary and Jesus to live in Nazareth in Galilee, which was bequeathed to Archelaus' younger brother Antipas. Referred to as "that fox" by

Jesus (Luke 13:31–32), Antipas was responsible for the death of John the Baptist.

Philip, son of Herod by Cleopatra, received the extreme northern territories of Batanea, Trachonitis, and Auranitis. Little is known about his rule, which was apparently uneventful and peaceful.

Herod Agrippa was the grandson of Herod the Great. He was raised in Rome and was awarded the territory of Judea and Samaria to rule in A.D. 41. He persecuted the early Christians. Under his brief rule, James, the son of Zebedee, was beheaded and Peter was imprisoned. Acts 12 relates how Agrippa was suddenly struck down while addressing a crowd in the theater at Caesarea in the year A.D. 44.

The last of the Herodian dynasty to rule in Judea was Agrippa's son, Agrippa II. In Acts 25, Paul appears before Agrippa II while imprisoned in Caesarea. Agrippa II sided with his Roman benefactors during the Jewish Revolt of A.D. 66–70, after which he thought it prudent to move to Rome, where he died sometime after A.D. 93.

Who Was in Charge of Whom?

I n 63 B.C., Pompey and his Roman legions put an end to the civil war in Judea. That date marked the beginning of centuries of Roman rule, which lasted throughout the period of the New Testament and early Church. Roman domination came to an end in the seventh century, when the Byzantines were defeated by Arab armies marching under the Islamic crescent.

In the time of Augustus, the ruling emperor when Jesus was born, the Roman Empire had an estimated population of between 70 and 90 million, spread out across much of the known world. All of this required efficient administration, at which Augustus excelled. He established major reforms that brought stability to Roman politics and society.

The three major institutions of ancient Rome were the emperor, the Senate, and the army. Prior to Augustus, the emperor and the Senate had often been at odds. When Julius Caesar assumed dictatorial powers, he attempted to abolish the Senate, who fled to

Augustus was emperor when Jesus was born.

Greece. Augustine trimmed the size of the Senate and appointed new members, but also granted it new powers.

It was not possible to become emperor without the allegiance of the army, yet every emperor was wary of his generals. This proved to be the undoing of many a Roman commander, including Mark Anthony and Pompey before him.

The Senate now had jurisdiction over one group of provinces, which were closer to home and peaceful. The imperial provinces, on the other hand, were farther away and required a military pres-

Legions in Judea

Roman legions were not stationed in Judea until the First Jewish Revolt. Only after suppressing the uprising were they permanently stationed in the land.

When they were not at war, the Roman legions in effect became construction battalions. The remains of their presence and work can still be seen. Legion X Fretensis took part in the conquest of Jerusalem by Titus in A.D. 70 and established its headquarters there. Many fragments of tiles have been found in the Old City stamped with the initials of this legion.

The emperor Hadrian sent several legions to put down the Second Jewish Revolt of A.D. 132–135. This revolt was even more violent than the First Revolt. Historians note that at this same time an entire Roman legion—the 25th from Egypt—disappeared from history. When the commander of the legions made his customary report to the Senate upon his return to Rome, instead of the customary greeting, "The emperor and the legions are well," he could only state, "The emperor is well."

The Legion X Fretensis took part in that campaign and afterward constructed a number of public works projects commissioned by the emperor Hadrian. The most enduring of these is an impressive aqueduct extending from Caesarea, some 15 miles north, to springs in the Haifa range; parts of it can still be seen today. An inscription attached to the aqueduct reads: "Imperator Caesar Traianus Hadrianus Augustus has made (this aqueduct) by a detachment of Legion X Fretensis."

Evidently, the Tenth Legion was aided in this massive construction project by another legion. At Megiddo, in the valley of Esdraelon, not far from the northern end of the aqueduct, an ancient village named el-Lejjun preserves the name "Legion." The remains of a Roman camp were located nearby; another telltale tile stamped with the abbreviation "LEGVIF" for Legio VI Ferrata, was found there.

ence. In this, Augustine shrewdly kept the upper hand. By directly administrating the provinces where the armies were, he maintained control over that vital institution.

At any given time, Rome fielded numerous legions scattered throughout the empire as needed. Each legion consisted of six thousand men—on paper at least—and was composed of ten cohorts of six hundred men each, more or less the equivalent of the modern battalion. In Acts 10:1, Cornelius is described as "a centurion of the Italian Cohort, as it was called."

The commander of a cohort was called a tribune, one of which (Claudius Lysias) is mentioned by name in Acts 23. The centurion, an officer in command of a hundred or more soldiers, completed the chain of command in the Roman army. Centurions were usually chosen from among the ranks for their courage and reliability. Several centurions are mentioned in the Gospels and Acts. Curiously, each is presented in a positive light, which is more than could be said about many Jewish leaders.

Did Ancient Judeans Sail to America?

cholars have long believed that, apart from a Viking settlement in Newfoundland, the first visitor to the New World was Christopher Columbus in 1492. However, a long-forgotten inscription discovered in 1889 might overturn that scholarly consensus. If genuine, the inscription is evidence of contact with the New World by mariners from ancient Judea.

The Smithsonian Institution's Institute of American Ethnology was conducting a survey of ancient mounds when it discovered a small inscribed stone in a mound next to the Little Tennessee River some 40 miles south of Knoxville. The mound contained nine skeletons lying in two parallel rows, all facing north except for one that faced south.

An inscription, measuring about 4.5 inches by 1.75 inches, was found under the skull of this skeleton. Also found were a pair of brass bracelets, the remains of jewelry, and some wood fragments—evidence that would prove crucial in dating the finds.

Eight characters were scratched on the stone, which came to be known as the Bat Creek Inscription. They were initially identified as letters of the Cherokee alphabet, said to have been

The Most Unusual Sea

The ancients were fascinated by the Dead Sea. We find mention of it in the writings of Aristotle, Strabo, Pliny the Younger, Tacitus, and others. This unique body of water lies on a giant crack in the Earth's surface stretching from Ethiopia to Turkey. At 1,300 feet below sea level, it is the deepest depression on the planet. By comparison, the lowest inhabited location in the United States, California's Death Valley, is 300 feet below sea level.

The water level of the Dead Sea has declined in recent years, and it is now divided into two separate bodies of water. The northern portion is yet another 1,300 feet deep, while the southern end is extremely shallow. The sea is void of all life, except for a highly adaptive microorganism only recently discovered by scientists. It has no outlet, and the evaporation of water through the ages has gradually intensified its salinity. At present, the water is saturated with various salts, the maximum being about 30 percent.

invented by a Cherokee in the 1820s. The only basis for this identification was the fact that the stone was found in historical
Cherokee territory.

For nearly 80 years, the Bat Creek Inscription lay forgotten
in a drawer at the National Museum of Natural History in Wash-
ington, D.C. Then, in the late 1960s, someone observed that the
text resembled Phoenician, the basis for the Canaanite and
Hebrew scripts.

A photo of the stone was sent to the Semitic languages
scholar Cyrus Gordon, who, after examining it, identified the
characters as a form of ancient Hebrew known as paleo-Hebrew.
Noting the resemblance to the writing on coins of the First and
Second Jewish Revolts against Rome, Gordon dated the inscription to the first or second century A.D. Even more remarkable was
Gordon's translation of the inscription: several of the letters
meant "for the Judeans."

The proposal that ancient Judeans may have visited the New
World was so radical that for two decades virtually no scholars
responded to the challenge posed by the Bat Creek Inscription.
But that silence was broken when new evidence regarding the
Bat Creek Inscription became available. The new evidence sur-
faced when the other artifacts found at Bat Creek were examined.

The pair of bracelets from the mound were originally thought
to be made of copper, which would not have been unusual for
ancient burial mounds. When Gordon announced his findings,
however, the Smithsonian Institution analyzed the metal and
found it was not copper, but heavily leaded yellow brass com-

posed of copper with approximately 27 percent zinc and 3.3 percent lead.

The 3.3 percent lead content prompted the Smithsonian to conclude that the bracelets could not have come from the time Gordon dated the Bat Creek Inscription. It was believed at the time that Roman brass of the first and second century A.D. never contained more than 1 percent lead. Subsequently, researchers at the British Museum demonstrated that brass with higher lead content was indeed widespread in the ancient world. Numerous ancient brass artifacts dated to the first and second century A.D. were found to contain essentially the same composition as the bracelets found at Bat Creek.

Significantly, production of brass with the higher lead content, such as found in the bracelets at Bat Creek, fell off after the second century A.D. This meant that if the bracelets found at Bat Creek were Judean, they would likely have been produced before 200 A.D. This coincides with the destruction of Judea by the Roman Emperor Hadrian after the Second Revolt in 135 A.D.

The crucial evidence for dating the findings at Bat Creek were the fragments of wood found along with the inscription and the bracelet. In 1970 the method of radiocarbon dating could not test the tiny fragments from Bat Creek. In more recent years, a new method of radiocarbon dating has been developed that requires only a few milligrams of carbon. The Smithsonian permitted the Bat Creek wood fragments to be tested.

As it turned out, the sample of material donated was not quite large enough to give the most accurate reading. However, scientists were able to date the wood to between 32 and 769 A.D.

Since the wood fragments were found with the bracelets in an undisturbed site, this suggests that the bracelets can be dated to before 200 A.D., which agrees with Cyrus Gordon's dating of the inscription to the first or second century A.D.

As the Little Tennessee River is not navigable beyond northern Alabama, the mystery remains as to how possible voyagers from Judea could have ended up at Bat Creek. Interestingly, it has been pointed out that the Judeans were not the only explorers to take such a route. Between 1539 and 1543, Hernando De Soto, one of the first explorers in the New World, crossed the Appalachians and traveled down the Tennessee River. The Spaniard is believed to have camped just 12 miles downstream from Bat Creek.

The identification of the Bat Creek artifacts as the remains of ancient Hebrew visitors to the New World has by no means convinced even a majority of scholars. The Bat Creek mound has long since been destroyed by plowing, and we may never know more about the strange group of travelers who may have found their way into the interior of America.

First-Century Ascetics

he Essenes were members of a Jewish sect that existed in Judea between the mid-second century B.C. to the end of the first century A.D. They numbered approximately 4,000 members—almost all males—who lived in monastic communities throughout the land.

The Essenes are believed to have originated in Babylon after the fall of Jerusalem. They reacted against what they saw as the moral laxity of the Jewish religious establishment and dedicated themselves to the strict observance of the Torah.

Scholars have pieced together the story of how the Essenes came to live in remote areas. Some scholars believe the settlement at Qumran near the shores of the Dead Sea, was an Essene community. After the successful Maccabean revolt of 167–164 B.C., some Essenes returned to Judea, bringing with them their ideas about religious reform. They were shocked by what they viewed as the compromise of pure Judaism on the part of the leaders of the rebuilt Temple. Their indignation won few converts, but one of these, who came to be known as the Teacher of Righteousness, was a member of the influential Sadok family, from whose ranks the High Priest had traditionally come.

The Teacher of Righteousness was already favorable toward the reforms that the Essenes advocated when he assumed the office of High Priest between 159 and 152 B.C. However, the hopes of the Essenes were dashed when he was deposed by the Jewish leader, Jonathan. After losing the power struggle in Jerusalem, the Teacher of Righteousness joined the Essenes and soon became their leader.

Some of the writings of the Teacher of Righteousness were preserved among the Dead Sea Scrolls found at Qumran. They portray him as a man of intense religious conviction who harbored deep resentment toward the religious establishment. He and his followers chose to live apart from Jewish society rather than endure what they viewed as its many corruptions.

The Essene Creed

The historian Josephus, who lived in Judea in the first century, was raised to be a rabbi—a Jewish religious teacher—and briefly joined the Essenes. He recorded the rigid vow that the Essenes took at the beginning of the common meal:

"Before touching the communal food, he must swear terrible oaths, first that he will revere the Godhead, and secondly that he will deal justly with men, will injure no one either of his own accord or at another's bidding, will always hate the wicked and cooperate with the good, and will keep faith at all times and with all men—especially with rulers, since all power is conferred by God. If he himself receives power, he will never abuse his authority and never by dress or additional ornament outshine those under him; he will always love truth and seek to convict liars, will keep his hands free from stealing and his soul innocent of unholy gain, and will never hide anything from members of the sect or reveal any of their secrets to others, even if brought by violence to the point of death. He further swears to impart their teaching to no man otherwise than as he himself received it, and take no part in armed robbery, and to preserve the books of the sect and in the same way the names of the angels. Such are the oaths by which they make sure of their converts." (Josephus, *The Jewish War,* II, 145.)

From Josephus we learn something of their strict way of life, which was marked by the avoidance of all luxuries and pleasures. The Essenes typically rose before dawn for prayers. After working in the morning, they dressed in linen garments and partook of a ritual bath. Afterward, they ate their midday meal, then worked until evening when they ate again in total silence.

Earning the full privilege of joining the sect required a probationary period of several years and the swearing of allegiance to the community. Upon becoming a member, the successful candidate was given the emblems of the community: a white robe and belt, along with a tool for digging holes in the earth when he relieved himself.

The law was central to the Essenes, and they studied it 24 hours a day in overlapping shifts of ten hours each. They were also preoccupied with the endless copying of biblical manuscripts and the writing of their own religious commentaries. Many of these documents, discovered hidden in caves along the Dead Sea, have furnished a wealth of information for historians and biblical scholars.

The Discovery of the Century?

 he first ancient scrolls at Qumran on the shores of the Dead Sea were discovered in 1947. The search of other caves in the cliffs along the sea was disrupted by war, as Israel and its neighbors fought over the territory where the first scrolls were found.

The fighting and subsequent political uncertainty over who would control the area did not prevent its native inhabitants, the Ta'amirah Bedouin, from engaging in their age-old profession of hunting for ancient artifacts to sell. Eventually, pieces of scrolls began showing up in the antiquities market, leading archaeologists to suspect that the Bedouin, who knew the area intimately, had found other scroll-bearing caves.

In 1952, Jordan's Department of Antiquities began a search of caves in the area, which led to the finding of "Cave 3." The chamber contained many fragments of leather scrolls similar to those found in other caves. Far more important, however, were the two rolls of copper found in a corner by themselves.

The two rolls—thin sheets of pure copper—turned out to be two halves of the same document, on which Hebrew script had been punched. Scholars were eager to read the scroll, but discovered quickly that it was too brittle to open.

The scholars, who were used to working with ancient scrolls made of leather and papyrus, were at a loss as to how to open the Copper Scroll. After deliberating for three years, they decided to

Qumran, site of the Dead Sea Scrolls.

send it to England, where it was painstakingly sawed into 23 sections and photographed.

As with many ancient artifacts, the Copper Scroll fared better during the nearly two thousand years it lay in the cave than it has in the decades since being removed. The scroll is composed of pure copper with only about one percent tin, which has prevented severe oxidation. Unfortunately, however, the edges have started to crumble, with some of the worst damage being on either side of the cuts.

Intent upon learning the secrets of the Copper Scroll, scholars set in motion the process of decay, which will eventually con-

sume it. Only time will tell if they will ever comprehend the
strange list of treasure locations contained in the document.

The Enigmatic Copper Scroll

 n 1952, in a cave near the barren shores of the Dead
Sea, the unique Copper Scroll was found. Unlike the
leather and papyrus manuscripts and fragments at
Qumran, the Copper Scroll, measuring around eight feet long
and eleven inches wide, is made of unusually pure copper.

The scroll dates to before the destruction of Jerusalem in
A.D. 70, and the Hebrew script in which it is written differs from
that of the other Qumran documents. Unlike the others, it is not
a religious document.

Rather, it appears to be an ancient treasure map. And not just
one map: The scroll details dozens of hiding places—64 to be
exact—containing fabulous quantities of treasure. The scroll
begins without introduction, listing the various locations, followed by the quantities of valuables at each one.

The sum total is staggering. Scholars estimate the amount of
silver, gold, and other valuables hidden to weigh between 58 and
174 tons. This initially caused many scholars to conclude that
the Copper Scroll was the result of some ancient scribe's over-
active imagination. But if fraudulent, it was a complex, costly
hoax. Copper was an expensive and almost unheard of material
to use in manuscripts. And why hide the scroll in a remote cave
where it would not be found for almost 2,000 years?

It has been pointed out that ancient documents from Jewish folklore—which few interpret literally—also describe the concealment of the treasure from the so-called First Temple. But these writings are very different, relating the legendary acts of famous figures such as Jeremiah in hiding the treasure.

By contrast, the Copper Scroll appears to be a no-nonsense, unembellished list that, unlike the others, does not include descriptions of any famous relics from the Jewish past. Accordingly, the scholarly consensus has cautiously come around to the possibility that the Copper Scroll is indeed describing locations where treasure is buried.

The various descriptions of the sites add to the mystery. The first location, for example, is "in the ruin that is in the Valley of Achor." It is thought that, in the first century, the Valley of Achor was north of Jericho in Wadi Nuwei'imeh. But what is the "ruin"? It may be the name of a village in the valley with a similar name.

The mystery deepens as the directions to the treasure are given: "Beneath the steps that enter to the east, forty cubits west: a chest of silver and its articles. Weight: 17 talents." Scholars disagree as to the weight of a talent at that time, with the possibilities ranging from 25 to 75 pounds. The second location is apparently near the first: "In the funerary shrine, in the third course of stones: 100 gold ingots." The mention of a funerary shrine suggests a town, perhaps no longer inhabited.

The third description suggests that another location is in view: "In the large cistern that is within the Court of the Peristylion, in a recess of its bottom, sealed in the entrenchment opposite the upper door: 900 talents." A peristyle is a small round courtyard surrounded by a colonnade. One would expect to see such a sophisticated structure in a larger metropolis like Jerusalem.

Some scholars have suggested that the third treasure location is somewhere inside the Temple Court. But if the purpose of the Scroll was to hide the treasure from the Romans, who were intent on conquering Jerusalem, it is unlikely that it would be hidden in the eye of the impending storm. (Indeed, the Temple was destined to be completely destroyed by Titus' legions.)

The Copper Scroll.

The list continues, identifying 64 locations around Judea said to contain large amounts of treasure. Some of the location descriptions have groups of Greek letters that scholars have been unable to interpret.

Further compounding the mystery is the last location listed on the scroll. Instead of treasure, this site is said to contain "a duplicate of this document and an explanation and their measurements and a precise reckoning of everything, one by one." It appears, then, that this second, duplicate scroll, which has not been found, may be necessary to interpret the descriptions of the other locations.

Adventurers have gone spade in hand throughout the land looking for the buried treasure. However, nothing has been found, not even in the most recognizable sites, such as the monument known as Absalom's tomb in the Kidron Valley of Jerusalem.

One intriguing theory is that the Copper Scroll is actually a list of tithes to the Temple treasury. The terms "contribution" and "tithe" appear throughout the scroll. In addition, at least one of the locations is on the estate of the priestly Hakkoz family, to whom was entrusted the Temple treasury after the exile. The fourth location reads: "In the cave that is next to the fountain belonging to the House of Hakkoz, dig six cubits. (There are) six bars of gold."

We find a reference to this family in the Book of Ezra that: "On the fourth day, within the house of our God, the silver, the gold, and the vessels were weighed into the hands of the priest Meremoth son of Uriah" (Ezra 8:33).

The Book of Nehemiah provides the final connection, referring to "Meremoth son of Uriah son of Hakkoz" (Nehemiah 3:4). Thus, the Hakkoz family mentioned in the Copper Scroll was responsible for the Temple treasury.

Jewish law specified that if the tithe could not be taken to Jerusalem for political or other reasons, it was to be stored in Genizah—a hidden place for sacred objects. Judea was in extreme turmoil during the years of the First Revolt (66–70 A.D.), which falls within the accepted dating of the Copper Scroll. This would explain the reason for hiding the treasure in various locations rather than taking it to the Temple treasury.

The questions will probably not be solved until the codes in the scroll are deciphered or the elusive second scroll is found. Until then, the Copper Scroll will likely remain one of the most mysterious treasure maps of all time.

A Treasure Too Fabulous to Be True?

any scholars have begun to consider the possibility that the Copper Scroll is actually a genuine list of treasures hidden in Judea before the end of the First Revolt (66–70 A.D.). Some scholars have connected these riches with the treasury of Jerusalem's Temple. However, one issue remains to be considered: The apparent sheer volume of these treasures.

The scroll lists approximately 4,630 talents of gold and silver, with each talent weighing between 25 and 75 pounds, yielding a total of between 58 and 174 tons of precious metals. By modern standards, that seems like an incredible amount.

The evidence from ancient literature and inscriptions tells the story of a vastly different age when precious metals were used as currency and were hoarded by nations in great quantities. Some of these records refer to treasures seized by conquerors; others list the contents of national treasuries. Still others detail the tribute paid by one country to another—normally exacted in gold and other precious metals.

Surprisingly, when compared to quantities described in other ancient records, the amounts of precious metals listed in the Copper Scroll are not unthinkable for their day. If all of the precious metals described in the Copper Scroll were converted to gold according to their relative value, the total would come to 39 tons.

Greek historian Herodotus provides us with our first statistics regarding the wealth of the ancient world. He lists the annual income of Persian kings as 39 tons of gold, virtually the same amount of wealth as listed in the Copper Scroll. But there's more—much more.

The treasure that Alexander the Great found at the Persian capitals of Persepolis and Susa amounted to the equivalent of around 836 tons, dwarfing what is listed in the Copper Scroll. The treasury of Athens in 432 B.C. is said to have contained 21 tons of gold; while in 347 B.C., the equivalent of 127 tons of gold were found in the treasury at Delphi. Sizable amounts of precious metals are known to have existed in Judea during that period as well. Herod the Great is said to have left 3.3 tons of gold to Augustus Caesar and his cronies.

Certainly there is little chance that any of Herod's money made its way into the Temple treasury, but other significant sources of income remained. The Temple was, after all, a tax-collecting body, gathering tithes from the Jews year after year, century after century.

If the cryptic riddles contained in the Copper Scroll are ever deciphered, perhaps the many treasures it describes can still be found.

Who Lived at Qumran?

n 1947 the world was stunned by the discovery of ancient biblical manuscripts in caves along the north-west shores of the Dead Sea. In the search to find who concealed the scrolls, attention soon focused on the nearby ruins of Qumran, named after the dry gorge of the same name. It was not until 1953, several years after Israel's War of Independence, that the site would finally be excavated. From the beginning it was widely believed that the site was occupied by the Essenes, an austere Jewish monastic religious sect that was a reaction against the religious establishment in Jerusalem.

Archaeologists uncovered what they believed to be the rudiments of a religious community, including a "scriptorium," a room with a long table presumably used for copying the scrolls found in nearby caves, and a "refectory" used for communal meals.

Two mikvot (ritual baths) where the members performed ceremonial baths were found at Qumran. In recent years some scholars have rejected the identification of the Qumran as a quasi-monastic Essene community. These scholars point out that Josephus, the first-century Jewish historian who is one of our primary ancient sources for the Essenes, does not specifically say they had a community at Qumran.

One suggestion is that the site was a winter villa similar to those in nearby Jericho. During winter the wealthy in Jerusalem would escape the cold of the central hill country by going to Jericho with its mild climate. Supporting this thesis are the delicate blown glass; finely cut stone urns; painted pottery; and even elegant column bases found at Qumran. Such fineries, it is argued, would be out of place in a monastic community. But while poverty was obligatory for individual Essenes, the community itself acquired material goods. The expensive items may also have been donated to the community by wealthy patrons. In any event, almost all of the pottery used at Qumran, was of a cheap, common variety. The thousands of pieces of simply made eating and drinking ware found at the site scarcely constitute evidence of an affluent villa.

Ruins of Qumran, Israel.

Yet another idea is that Qumran was a military fortress. There is what appears to be a fortified tower at the site, and signs of battle have been found including Roman iron arrowheads from the destruction of the site in 68 A.D.

However, many structures—even farmhouses—had towers in ancient days. One can readily understand how an isolated religious community would provide for its own defense against marauding bands.

More damaging to the military fortress thesis is the fact that the settlement at Qumran has no outer defensive wall and is easily accessible from almost every side. The so-called fortified tower may simply be a two-story structure with strengthened walls.

The fortified tower may also be a "keep"; a common structure in ancient towns. A keep was a strong tower where the nobility—and, with any luck, many of the inhabitants of the city as well—could flee when the defenses of the city crumbled under attack. If so, the fortified tower at Qumran does not mean that the site was a military fort.

The death knell to the view that Qumran was either a villa or a military fortress is the scrolls themselves. Found in caves near the site, over 98 percent are religious in nature. What use would either a military fortress or a villa have for such a hoard? Furthermore, the vast cemetery adjoining the settlement would have been out of place in either a villa or a military fort. But it does fit with the original thesis that Qumran was a long-term community of about 200 people who lived their lives—and died—on a bleak plateau overlooking the Dead Sea.

Eating and Drinking at Qumran

Providing food and water in a desert presents challenges, which the Essenes met in resourceful ways. One of the excavated rooms, the communal dining room, sheds insight into how and what its inhabitants ate.

In an adjoining storeroom, more than 700 bowls were found, carefully arranged in piles of a dozen. Other assorted eating and drinking utensils, including 210 plates and 75 beakers, were found here as well. Archaeologists have pieced together that their diet consisted of bread, wine, and as the main course, a bowl of cooked meat. The meat was mutton, beef, or goat, and would usually be boiled but sometimes roasted. Curiously, the leftover bones were carefully buried after being covered with broken pieces of pottery. This suggests that some meals had a ritual significance.

In a desert area such as the region of the Dead Sea, obtaining sufficient quantities of water is a concern of utmost importance. Qumran solved the problem with an ingenious system that included a dam, an aqueduct, and cisterns.

Unlike the bone-dry region around the Dead Sea, the hill country of Judea received significant precipitation during the winter months. After a particularly heavy rainfall, the water would drain into the normally dry wadi systems running down to the Dead Sea. These would fill with water, in some cases turning into raging torrents as they raced down to the sea, located thirteen hundred feet below sea level.

Qumran lay on a plateau at the head of one of one of these gorges, known as Wadi Qumran. Above the settlement, a dam was built across the wadi, which would fill with water during these infrequent flash floods. The water that accumulated was diverted into an aqueduct leading to Qumran, where it filled cisterns that supplied the community with water throughout the year.

This water system was quite sophisticated. A filtration pool was built into the aqueduct to remove the fine sand that would otherwise clog the system. The sand sank to the bottom, while the clear water flowed into the system of channels that diverted water throughout the settlement.

The water system also served the ritual baths known as Mikvot. The Essenes were required to perform ritual baths before entering the "holy temple" of the refectory.

The excavation at Qumran uncovered no living quarters. Where, then, did the Essenes live? Given their austere lifestyle, it is assumed they inhabited the numerous caves in the vicinity, or that they lived in tents or other temporary shelters.

Archaeologists excavated a "scriptorium" where the Essene scribes would copy their sacred manuscripts. Two inkwells containing dried ink were found among the debris of this room. The settlement also contained a complete pottery workshop, including a circular pit for the potter's wheel, and kilns for firing the earthenware. The large jars in which some of the scrolls were found were likely made here.

When they completed their work on earth, the members of the community were buried in a nearby cemetery. Of those excavated, the vast majority are adult males. The severity of their life is indicated by an average life span of less than 40 years.

THE PIVOTAL PERSON
What Is Anointing?

he Hebrew word "messiah" means to "smear" or "anoint." The high priest Aaron (brother of Moses and Miriam) and his sons were consecrated to the priesthood by being anointed with oil. Saul, the first king of Israel, was called "the anointed of the Lord"—a title that became synonymous with "king."

Little is known about the method of anointing. According to Jewish tradition, olive oil was poured on the head and rubbed on the forehead in the form of a cross. The anointing signified that the priest or king was endowed with the Spirit of God and that he was chosen by God to fill his office.

Unlike rulers of other cultures in the ancient Near East, the Israelite kings never claimed divine honors. There was, however, a transformation that took place when the king was anointed. At the anointing of Saul, we read that "after [Saul] turned away to leave Samuel, God gave him another heart; and all these signs were fulfilled that day. When they were going from there to Gibeah, a band of prophets met him; and the spirit of God possessed him, and he fell into a prophetic frenzy along with them" (1 Samuel 10:9–10).

Through disobedience, Saul forfeited his anointing, and the Lord chose a new king. Samuel was sent to Bethlehem, and after finding David "took the horn of oil, and anointed him in the presence of his brothers; and the spirit of the Lord came mightily upon David from that day forward" (1 Samuel 16:13).

Saul, however, still ruled, and his antagonism toward David grew into open, murderous hostility. David was forced to flee with his compatriots to the wilderness of En-Gedi. But respect

for the one who had been anointed was so ingrained in David that when he had the opportunity to kill Saul he refused, saying, "The Lord forbid that I should do this thing to my lord, the Lord's anointed, to raise my hand against him; for he is the Lord's anointed" (1 Samuel 24:6).

Saul is anointed by Samuel.

David's son and successor, Solomon, failed to observe another requirement of those anointed by the Lord— to rule with care as a shepherd cares for his sheep: "And he shall stand and feed his flock in the strength of the Lord" (Micah 5:4). Solomon's grandiose building projects and his greatly expanded empire required high taxes, forced labor, and military conscription, which violated this.

The ideal of anointing was never fully realized in any of the kings of Judah or Israel. It would be left to one who was yet to come, the future Messiah, who would become the fulfillment of the Anointed One.

When Was Jesus Born?

he Gregorian calendar, instituted by Pope Gregory XIII in 1582, and still used for civil purposes around the world today, is correct to within one day in 20,000 years. However, the pivotal date of the Gregorian calendar—the birth of Jesus Christ—cannot be fixed with precision. We do know that it is incorrect by several years.

The Gospels provide several historical details about the life of Christ that help establish the dates of his birth and death—but only broadly. We read in the Gospel of Luke that the events of Jesus' birth occurred "in the days of King Herod of Judea" (Luke 1:5). The Herod that Luke is referring to, known as "Herod the Great," ruled Judea from 37 B.C. to his death in 4 B.C. Since Herod was alive when Jesus was born, we know that Jesus could not have been born after 4 B.C.—after Herod's death.

A further clue is found in the Gospel of Matthew: "In the time of King Herod, after Jesus was born in Bethlehem of Judea, wise men from the East came to Jerusalem, asking, 'Where is the child who has been born king of the Jews? For we observed his star at its rising, and have come to pay him homage.' When Herod the king heard this, he was troubled . . ." (Matthew 2:1–2). A few verses later we learn that Herod met with the travelers from the East, "Then Herod secretly called for the wise men and learned from them the exact time when the star had appeared . . ." (Matthew 2:7).

Presumably, Herod did not receive the Wise Men in his final months, when he had become deathly ill and was preoccupied with finding a cure for his various ailments. If we assume that the wise men arrived in Jerusalem a year or so before Herod's death, that would place the birth of Jesus at between 7 and 5 B.C.

A Star in the East

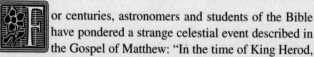 or centuries, astronomers and students of the Bible have pondered a strange celestial event described in the Gospel of Matthew: "In the time of King Herod, after Jesus was born in Bethlehem of Judea, wise men from the East came to Jerusalem, asking, 'Where is the child who has been born king of the Jews? For we observed his star at its rising, and have come to pay him homage.'... Then Herod secretly called for the wise men and learned from them the exact time when the star had appeared... When they had heard the king, they set out; and there, ahead of them, went the star that they had seen at its rising, until it stopped over the place where the child was" (Matthew 2:7–9).

Identification of the star is complicated by the uncertainties over when Jesus was born, which is generally estimated as occurring between the years 8 and 4 B.C. In those years, several celestial events of note took place that various scholars suggest may have been the "star" that the wise men saw.

One theory is that the star was none other than Halley's Comet, which would have been visible in the fall of 12 B.C. It is thought that the tail of the comet helped to "point" the way toward Bethlehem. However, in the ancient Near East, comets were considered evil omens, not signs of good tidings, as the birth of Jesus was intended to be. It is also difficult to imagine how Halley's Comet would have pointed to Bethlehem.

Another explanation for the star was the possible sighting of the planet Jupiter near the star Regulus. Astrologers in ancient Mesopotamia considered Jupiter to be the "king" planet. Since Regulus also means "king," the conjunction of the two would have been significant. Also, Regulus is in the constellation Leo, which is the astrological sign of the ancient tribe of Judah. This conjunction, however, occurred a year after the death of Herod the Great and may be too late to fit the chronology of the nativity story.

Another possibility was first suggested by the seventeenth-century astronomer Johann Kepler. He correctly calculated that three alignments of Jupiter and Saturn occurred in 7 B.C. Astronomers now know that the first one took place in May of that year. This would have been a highly significant event, considering that Saturn is the ruling planet of Judah. Also, the alignment took place in the constellation Pisces, known as "The House of the Hebrews."

Even more momentous was a near-alignment of Mars, Jupiter, and Saturn in September of 6 B.C. This is a rare event, occurring only once every 800 years.

One final possibility comes from records kept by Chinese astronomers, who reported a new star in the constellation Capricorn in the spring of 5 B.C. This star—likely a nova—was visible for 70 days, appearing several hours before sunrise in the East. However, this location would have been the opposite of

Matthew's star, which guided the wise men; they came "from the East" and journeyed westward.

The suggested theories for the identity of the star, while intriguing, remain to varying degrees unsatisfactory, for they fail to account for the star's precise guidance of the wise men to Bethlehem. Thus, there remains the possibility that the star was part of a miraculous event, apart from these natural phenomena.

When Was Jesus Crucified?

etermining when Jesus was crucified is complicated by the uncertainties over when Jesus was born. In the broadest terms, this was probably between 8 and 4 B.C. The next data, which is also controversial, concerns the length of Jesus' earthly ministry.

Luke, a physician who traveled with Paul, wrote about the life of Jesus in the Gospel that carries his name, and in the Book of Acts. The Book of Luke, thought to be written around 70 A.D., tells us: "Jesus was about thirty years old when he began his work" (Luke 3:23). In addition, at least three Passovers (celebrated once a year) are mentioned in the Gospels as having taken place during Jesus' ministry. This would indicate a life span of about 33 years.

But another historical detail is recorded in Luke. John the Baptist began his ministry "in the fifteenth year of the reign of Emperor Tiberius, when Pontius Pilate was governor of Judea, and Herod was ruler of Galilee" (Luke 3:1). [The "Herod" mentioned here is not Herod the Great, but his son Antipas, who ruled in Galilee and who inherited the title "Herod."] The fifteenth year of the Emperor Tiberius was in A.D. 28–29.

John's baptism of Jesus that year marked the beginning of Jesus' ministry. As already mentioned, the Gospels report at least three, possibly four, Passovers. Still other scholars maintain that the period of Jesus' ministry was actually one year rather than three.

Obviously, the exact year eludes all the various scholars. What we do know for sure is that the crucifixion of Jesus took place between A.D. 28 and 29, which is when Pontius Pilate was praefect of Judea.

When Is Jesus' Birthday?

hristmas, with its wintry manger scenes in straw-filled wooden barns, provides endearing images. But in light of historical and biblical evidence, these recreations are somewhat fanciful.

The New Testament does not give the time of year when Jesus was born. We do, however, have one clue suggesting that the time of year could not have been winter. The Gospel of Luke states that, "In that region there were shepherds living in the fields, keeping watch over their flock by night" (Luke 2:8). In Palestine, the grain crops are grown in winter during the rainy season. Animals are not permitted in the fields during the growing season because they would trample the stalks. After the grain is harvested, the sheep and goats are allowed to graze the stubble and fertilize the fields.

The birth of Jesus was first celebrated December 25 in the fourth century. Up until then, December 25 marked the weeklong revelry of the Saturnalia, one of the most popular festivals of ancient Rome. The festival was a celebration of the winter solstice, which occurs on December 21. After the empire became Christianized, the pagan festival was transformed into a Christian holiday.

The familiar nativity picture of Joseph and Mary being turned away from the inn at Bethlehem is likewise inaccurate. We read in the Gospel of Luke that Mary delivered Jesus and laid him in a manger "because there was no place for them in the inn" (Luke 2:7).

The Greek word that was translated as "inn" actually means a "guest room" or "dining room." Luke uses the word only one other time—in his description of the Last Supper. The word he uses for the "guest room" in which they celebrated the Passover, elsewhere described as a "large room upstairs, already furnished" (Luke 22:11–12), is the same Greek word used in the story of Mary and Joseph.

There would have been walled enclosures in the countryside where shepherds and travelers could find shelter with their animals. But hotels or inns would have been unknown in first-century Judea. People traveled infrequently, and when they did, they would plan to stay with relatives.

The one exception was Jerusalem, whose population could double during the Passover feast. Those who had no relatives in the city to stay with made other arrangements for lodging. It is in this context that we read about the "guest room" that Jesus and his disciples used to celebrate their Passover.

The reason for Mary and Joseph's trip to Bethlehem was to register for the census decreed by Caesar Augustus. This meant that the town was filled with travelers like themselves, who were returning to their place of origin for the census.

It is likely that, upon arriving in Bethlehem, Joseph and Mary went to their relatives looking for lodging. However, the "guest room" was occupied, perhaps by visitors more distinguished than they. It is also possible that their prospective hosts did not realize how far along Mary was in her pregnancy.

We are not told exactly where they ended up staying. That the newborn babe Jesus was placed in a "manger"—a stone feeding trough—indicates they found shelter with the animals.

A painting of Mary and Jesus by Stefan Lochner.

It is not likely that this was a massive-beamed barn like that portrayed by northern European artists. Even today, the area around Bethlehem has many caves used to shelter animals. In those times, homes in Palestine were often built over natural caves that were enlarged to provided a secure place for animals to stay. And, some homes were built with a separate first-floor area where animals were kept.

It is likely that Mary and Joseph were offered a place in one of these interior "stables" by their apologetic hosts, who had nothing else to offer.

THE GOSPELS
Israel: The Fifth Gospel?

srael has been called the "fifth gospel" because this land is the key to understanding much of the background of Bible stories.

Packed into this relatively small country, measuring approximately 150 miles by 50 miles, is an amazing diversity that few regions can match. The elevation varies from 9,200 feet on the snow-covered peaks of Mount Hermon to the barren deserts next to the Dead Sea at 1,300 feet below sea level. The vegetation at En-Gedi along the shores of the Dead Sea is subtropical, but a few hundred meters above in the wilderness of Judea, only a few hardy plants can be found in the sun-washed desert.

Students of the Bible have wondered why the tiny land of Israel has been the attention of so many empires. The location provides the answer. Israel is on the land bridge between three continents: Africa, Asia, and Europe. For that reason, Israel has experienced the cultures and armies of these regions, whose exploits in the Holy Land are recounted in the Bible and in many other texts from antiquity.

The Assyrians and Babylonians came from the continent of Asia, the Egyptians from Africa, and the Greeks and Romans from Europe. They traveled along the same ancient trade routes that the biblical characters used.

Unlike the great river cultures of Egypt and Mesopotamia, the land of Israel depends on the seasonal rains for water. Rainfall can vary from up to 40 inches in northern Galilee to only a few inches annually in the southern deserts.

It never needed to rain in Egypt and Mesopotamia; thus their chief deities, Amon Re and Marduk, were sun gods. By comparison, the chief god of Canaan was Baal, a god of rain and fertility often pictured with a lightning bolt in his upraised arm.

As the Israelites prepared to enter Canaan, the land was described to them: "... the land that you are about to enter to occupy is not like the land of Egypt, from which you have come, where you sow your seed and irrigate by foot like a vegetable garden. But the land you are about to enter is a land of hills and valleys, watered by rain from the sky, a land that the Lord your God looks after" (Deuteronomy 11:10–12).

In ancient Egypt, farmers irrigated their crops using pumps that brought the waters of the Nile into their fields. The inhabitants of Israel did not have the luxury of an abundant supply of water. As the text of Deuteronomy indicates, the Israelites were to look to the God of Heaven for their survival.

The drama of the Bible is played out against this relationship. It is largely a tragic story, as Israel became increasingly rebellious rather than continue their dependence on God. Even the land itself sought in vain to teach them.

Messianic Candidates

he age into which Jesus was born was one of heightened expectation of the coming Messiah. The Jewish people eagerly awaited their coming king, who would put an end to Roman domination and bring about the spiritual renewal of their nation.

Several Messiah candidates are mentioned in the New Testament and in the writings of the contemporary Jewish historian Josephus. The first of these was John the Baptist, who began preaching and baptizing in the region of the Jordan River. We read that the crowds of people who came out to see him were "filled with expectation, and all were questioning in their hearts concerning John, whether he might be the Messiah" (Luke 3:15).

John baptizes his cousin Jesus.

John steadfastly denied that he was the Messiah, telling the people: "I baptize you with water; but one who is more powerful than I is coming; I am not worthy to untie the thong of his sandals" (Luke 3:16).

Another Messianic figure named Theudas appeared on the scene after the time of Jesus, during the rule of the procurator

Cuspius Fadus (A.D. 44–46). According to Josephus, Theudas led a large crowd to the Jordan River, where he promised to repeat Joshua's miracle by commanding the river to dry up, after which he would lead his followers across.

Fadus sent a squadron of cavalry against the fanatics, who were gathered on the riverbank waiting for the miracle to transpire. Many were taken prisoner, and their leader Theudas was killed. His severed head was brought back to Jerusalem.

This episode is also mentioned in the Book of Acts, where the Pharisee Gamaliel cautions his fellow members of the Sanhedrin against taking extreme action against the Apostle Peter: "Fellow Israelites, consider carefully what you propose to do to these men. For some time ago Theudas rose up, claiming to be somebody, and a number of men, about four hundred, joined him; but he was killed, and all who followed him were dispersed and disappeared" (Acts 5:35).

In his speech, Gamaliel gave another example of a false Messiah: "After him Judas the Galilean rose up at the time of the census and got people to follow him; he also perished, and all who followed him were scattered" (Acts 5:37). Josephus mentions Jacob and Simeon, the sons of Judah the Galilean, who attempted to lead a revolt under the procurator Tiberius Alexander (A.D. 46–48). Alexander had both of the sons of Judah crucified.

Josephus records that, under the procurator Felix (A.D. 52–59), an unnamed Egyptian gathered thousands of disciples. They followed him up to the Mount of Olives, where he promised to bring down the walls of Jerusalem and deliver the Roman garrison into their hands. The Egyptian promised to then rule as king over the nation. Felix sent soldiers against them, massacring many, but their leader managed to escape, never to be heard from again.

This event is mentioned in Acts, when the Apostle Paul is being arrested in the courtyard of the Temple. The Roman commander suspects Paul is the Egyptian who got away. Then, after he hears Paul speak Greek, the commander remarks: "Then you are not the Egyptian who recently stirred up a revolt and led the four thousand assassins out into the wilderness?" (Acts 21:38).

Finally, Josephus also reports that, during the rule of the procurator Festus, an anonymous self-styled prophet promised salvation to all who would follow him into the desert. Soldiers were dispatched to dispel the gathered crowds with force, killing the prophet along with a number of his followers.

The Jewish people longed for a Messiah who would bring political liberation from the Romans. This is apparent in the large number of people who followed would-be Messiah figures in the hope of finding some peace.

Throughout Jesus' ministry, many hoped Jesus would be the political Messiah they were waiting for. The Gospel of John records what happened when Jesus explained the profoundly spiritual nature of his ministry: "Because of this many of his disciples turned back and no longer went about with him" (John 6:66).

Their hopes would not die, though. As Jesus was approaching Jerusalem the week of his arrest, the people laid down palm branches, a Jewish messianic symbol, on the path before him.

They paid no heed to what he tried to tell them: "My kingdom is not of this world."

Where Is Herod's Tomb?

erod the Great was a name bestowed upon himself by the notorious monarch. Among his grandiose building projects was a series of fortresses in the wilderness. These strongholds were not constructed to protect against foreign invasion, for Herod faced few if any external threats.

Rather, the fortresses served primarily for Herod's personal protection. During his long reign, Herod made many enemies among his Judean subjects, and the fortresses served as refuges to flee to in the event of an attempted coup in Jerusalem.

One of Herod's most impressive desert strongholds is the Herodium, visible today as a lone, flat-topped mountain on the edges of the wilderness east of Bethlehem. The site held nostalgic value for the Idumean king: In 40 B.C., Herod's political opponents in Jerusalem took advantage of a Parthian invasion of nearby Syria to stir revolt in Judea. Forced to flee for his life with his immediate family, Herod fought a rear-guard battle at the site.

During the fight, his mother was critically injured when her chariot overturned. Fearing that her injuries were fatal, Herod tried to commit suicide but was restrained. Herod and his entourage made it safely to Masada. While his mother recovered, Herod made his way to Rome, where he was proclaimed King of the Jews.

The memory of this battle and his mother's near-fatal accident so impressed Herod that 20 years later he returned to build a fortress on the site of the earlier battle. As usual, Herod spared no expense to make Herodium another of his impressive construction projects. To increase the height of the hill on which the

fortress was built, he leveled a nearby hill and added the rubble to the base of the Herodium.

On top of the artificial mountain, he constructed cylindrical walls seven stories high with four massive towers. The

Masada may be King Herod's burial site.

tallest, which served as Herod's private keep, had three levels of living space and soared a hundred feet above the walls. The Herodium was equipped with the usual Roman amenities to which Herod had become accustomed, including a bathhouse, a columned hall, and dining room. On the grounds below, a lavish palace was constructed, complete with a swimming pool and formal Roman-style gardens.

Of all the sites of his building projects around the land of Judea, it is the barren wilderness setting of the Herodium that Herod chose for his burial. Josephus describes Herod's last agonizing days as he sought relief from his various maladies at the hot springs of Machaerus on the eastern shores of the Dead Sea before succumbing at his palace at Jericho. An elaborate funeral procession accompanied Herod's solid gold bier to the Herodium, where, according to Josephus, Herod was interred.

For archaeologists, the mystery of where he was buried is one that is very much alive. Beginning in the 1970s, the Herodium has been systematically excavated. Archaeologists hoped to find the tomb of Herod but were puzzled when they found no remains that resembled a royal tomb.

A likely place for the tomb of Herod was the round tower that served as his keep, but initial examination determined that the base was solid. However, that conclusion has recently been challenged with the use of new techniques for discovering hidden chambers.

The Burial of Herod

Josephus records how Archelaus, the newly proclaimed king of Judea, attended to the burial of his father:

"Everything possible was done by Archelaus to add to the magnificence: He brought out all the royal ornaments to be carried in procession in honor of the dead monarch. There was a solid gold bier, adorned with precious stones and draped with the richest purple. On it lay the body wrapped in crimson, with a diadem resting on the head and above that a golden crown, and the sceptre by the right hand. The bier was escorted by Herod's sons and the whole body of his kinsmen, followed by his spearmen, the Thracian Company, and his Germans and Gauls, all in full battle order, headed by their commanders and all the officers, and followed by five hundred of the house slaves and freedmen carrying spices. The body was borne twenty-four miles to Herodium, where by the late king's command it was buried. So ends the story of Herod."

The tower was examined using two different sensing technologies, geophysical radar and ground-penetrating sonar devices, both of which indicated a chamber 8 to 10 feet in diameter inside the tower. The same high-technology sensing equipment discovered unexplored subterranean chambers underneath a building at the base of the Herodium. Fragments of beautifully carved stones, which might have been part of a mausoleum, were found in this area.

It may be that Herod's tomb was looted and destroyed in the centuries after his reign and that nothing remains to be found. Technical difficulties and financial constraints have prevented the excavation of these newly discovered chambers. Archaeologists still dream of finding the solid gold bier and other treasures buried with the infamous "King of the Jews."

The Man and His Mission

We read in the Gospel of Luke that the enraged inhabitants of Nazareth tried to throw Jesus off a cliff after he applied a prophecy of Isaiah to himself: "The Spirit of the Lord is on me, because he has anointed me to preach good news to the poor. He has sent me to proclaim freedom for the prisoners and recovery of sight for the blind, to release the oppressed, to proclaim the year of the Lord's favor" (Luke 4:18–19).

Some see Jesus' use of this passage—which speaks of "freedom for the prisoners" and releasing the oppressed—as a manifesto for insurrection against the heavy-handed Roman occupation of Palestine. Indeed, many in Jesus' day were looking for a messiah figure who would lead such a revolt. History records several messiah figures, including Judas Maccabeus and Bar Kochba, who led the Jewish people in bloody uprisings.

However, Jesus steadfastly refused to allow himself to be cast as a political messiah. He rebuked those who came to arrest him in the Garden of Gethsemane: "Am I leading a rebellion, that you have come with swords and clubs?" (Luke 22:52).

Later, when questioned by Pontius Pilate as to whether he considered himself to be the king of the Jews, he replied: "My kingdom is not of this world. If it were, my servants would fight to prevent my arrest by the Jews ... my kingdom is from another place" (John 18:36).

If, by quoting Isaiah, Jesus was not advocating revolution, then what was he talking about? We find the key in another response of Jesus when questioned about the kingdom of God: "The kingdom of God does not come visibly, nor will people say, 'Here it is,' or 'There it is,' because the kingdom of God is within you" (Luke 17:20–21). Jesus was saying that his mission on earth was primarily a spiritual one. His intent was not to lead a political revolt but to revolutionize hearts.

After his rejection in Nazareth, we have no indication in the Gospels that Jesus ever returned there. From then on, Capernaum is referred to as Jesus' "home" (Mark 2:1) and "his own town" (Matthew 9:1). Capernaum, along with Korazin on the heights above the water, and nearby Bethsaida, form what Bible scholars call the "evangelical triangle"—the geographical region

Area of Jesus' ministry.

where Jesus conducted much of his ministry.

Jesus' ministry did not have the intended effect in this region either: "Then Jesus began to denounce the cities in which most of his miracles had been performed, because they did not repent. 'Woe to you, Korazin! Woe to you Bethsaida! If the miracles that were performed in you had been performed in Tyre and Sidon, they would have repented long ago in sackcloth and ashes.... And you, Capernaum, will you be lifted up to the skies? No, you will go down to the depths. If the miracles that were performed in you had been performed in Sodom, it would have remained to this day. But I tell you that it will be more bearable for Sodom on the day of judgment than for you" (Matthew 11:21, 23–24).

Jesus wanted his miracles to have a life-transforming effect on those who experienced them. Sadly, all too often this was not the case. Given the large number of miracles that the Gospels say he performed, and given the rather small geographic area of Galilee, there could not have been many extended families that were not touched by Jesus' ministry.

Yet many rejected Jesus' message, fulfilling his proverb that "a prophet has no honor in the prophet's own country" (Luke 4:24).

How Did Herod Build Caesarea Maritima?

he story of Caesarea Maritima is shrouded in intrigue. In 31 B.C., Octavian—who was given the name Augustus by decree of the Roman Senate—completed his revenge on the murderers of Julius Caesar by defeating Marc Anthony at the Battle of Actium.

King Herod of Judea had supported Anthony up until then, but had an uncanny ability to curry favor with whoever was in power in Rome. He wasted no time in switching allegiances, traveling to Rome laden with gifts for the new emperor.

Perhaps because he was impressed with the gall of the upstart Herod, Augustus decided he was just the man to look out for his interests in the defiant land of Judea, which had come under direct Roman control in 63 B.C.

Besides being one of the cruelest taskmasters the Jews ever had, Herod the Great was a shrewd businessman. He realized that the local spices and other agricultural products could sell for three or four times the normal price in Rome. He only had to get there before the Egyptian ships that sailed from Alexandria in the spring. Unfortunately, there was no serviceable natural harbor along the whole of the coast of Judea.

Not being one to let obstacles stand in his way, Herod decided to build a port. He named his new city Caesarea Maritima in honor of Augustus. The addition of "Maritima" was necessary to distinguish the city from Caesarea Philippi at the foot of Mount Hermon in northern Israel. One of Herod the Great's most ambitious building projects, Caesarea was the first artificially created port in the ancient world. It required the creation of a massive breakwater that extended nearly a third of a mile out into the sea.

Two developments in the ancient world made the building of such a port possible. Roman engineers invented a waterproof concrete that hardened underwater. The ingredient that made this possible was a volcanic sand known as pozzolana, a bonding agent similar to portland cement.

Cleopatra at the Battle of Actium.

Then, in 25 B.C., a few years before Herod began building Caesarea, a Roman engineer and architect named Vitruvius published a treatise entitled "On Architecture." Vitruvius' book set forth the "state of the art" in Roman architecture and discussed, among other things, harbor construction. It is likely that Herod's engineers had access to this book.

The city had the usual amenities that expatriate Romans favored, including a theater seating several thousand and a stadium for racing horses. Caesarea even boasted a sewer system designed to flush each day with the tides. Blocks of warehouses stored local produce until it could be loaded for shipment to Rome.

Several significant incidents in the New Testament occurred in Caesarea. Herod Agrippa was struck down in the theater here, and the Apostle Peter was sent here to the Roman Centurion Cornelius, who would later become the first Gentile convert to the new Christian faith. The Apostle Paul passed through Caesarea several times, staying at the home of Philip the Evangelist, before being imprisoned and sent to Rome.

At the onset of the First Jewish Revolt in A.D. 66, tensions between Jews and Gentiles led to the desecration of the synagogue in Caesarea. Josephus records that 20,000 Jews were killed in the ensuing riots.

From Caesarea, revolt spread around the land until Vespasian, sent from Rome, arrived with his legions to regain the land. Later, when his son Titus completed the subjugation of Judea, he returned to Caesarea with Jewish captives. During the victory celebrations, 2,500 of these prisoners perished in gladiatorial games in the theater.

Is This the House of St. Peter?

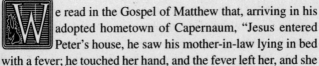 e read in the Gospel of Matthew that, arriving in his adopted hometown of Capernaum, "Jesus entered Peter's house, he saw his mother-in-law lying in bed with a fever; he touched her hand, and the fever left her, and she got up and began to serve him" (Matthew 8:14–15).

Excavations at Capernaum have uncovered a number of enclosed dwellings called *insuli,* which accommodated extended families of up to 100 persons. These were large walled areas composed of rooms surrounding a central courtyard. Archaeologists believe they may have found the *insuli* that housed Peter's extended family.

One of the enclosed dwellings contained a room that was set apart from the others. Dating to the first century A.D., it was the only room at Capernaum to have plastered floors and walls. At least six layers of plastered pavements were found, indicating that the area was well-used over an extended period of time. It is thought that religious gatherings took place in this room.

Late in the fourth century, a wall was built around this room. Christian graffiti was found on plaster chunks that had fallen face down from this wall—including the names Jesus, God, and Christ. Liturgical expressions such as

Heems Kerr's painting of Peter preaching.

Amen and *kyrie eleison* were also found, as was the name Peter.

Interestingly, the presence of different languages indicates the site was a place of pilgrimage. The Spanish Sister Egeria wrote in 384 that "in Capernaum the house of the prince of the apostles has been made into a church, with its original walls still standing." By the fifth century, an octagonal church was built over the site, prompting a visitor to write in 570 that "the house of St. Peter is now a basilica."

That structure was eventually destroyed, and Capernaum lay abandoned until excavations in our time have once again brought the ancient site of Peter's house to light.

The Jesus Boat

n 1986, the Sea of Galilee was at its lowest level in memory. At this time, archaeologists identified a number of previously unknown anchorages around the sea, indicating a thriving fishing industry in ancient times.

In January of that year, two brothers from Kibbutz Ginosar on the shores of the sea noticed the oval outline of what appeared to be a boat in a mud bar that had been exposed by the receding waters. News reports soon trumpeted the discovery of what was dubbed the "Jesus boat." Archaeologists dated it to between 100 B.C. and A.D. 100, declaring it the first ancient ship ever found in the Sea of Galilee.

The rising water level threatened to endanger the salvage operation as archaeologists sought the best means to remove the fragile remains from the seabed. Using new techniques in marine excavation and preservation, they encased the boat in polyurethane and floated it to shore.

The Sea of Galilee boat is almost certainly the same type with which Jesus and his disciples (some of whom were fishermen) would have been familiar. Twenty-six feet long and seven feet

wide, the boat is built with wooden joints, which is characteris-
tic of this period. It had been repaired on several occasions, indicating it had a long life.

Jesus was likely resting in the hold of such a boat in the
Gospel story of a storm on the Sea of Galilee: "A great wind-
storm arose, and the waves beat into the boat, so that the boat
was already being swamped. But he was in the stern, asleep on
the cushion; and they woke him up and said to him, 'Teacher,
do you not care that we are perishing?' He woke up and rebuked
the wind, and said to the sea, 'Peace! Be still!' Then the wind
ceased, and there was a dead calm" (Mark 4:37–39).

Ancient sources indicate that ships of this size had a crew of
five, including four rowers and a helmsman. Josephus refers to
ships of this size holding as many as 15 people. Jesus and his 12
disciples would have fit comfortably into such a boat.

There is no evidence connecting the Sea of Galilee boat
found at Kibbutz Ginosar with Jesus. He or his disciples may
have seen it or even ridden in it. Jesus' hometown was a few miles
north along the shore where the boat was found.

The Healing Pool

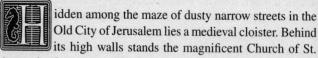 idden among the maze of dusty narrow streets in the
Old City of Jerusalem lies a medieval cloister. Behind
its high walls stands the magnificent Church of St.
Anne, the finest example of a Crusader church still standing in
the Holy Land.

Next to the church lie the impressive ruins of the ancient Pool of Bethesda spoken of in the Gospels. It is here where Jesus healed a man who had been an invalid for 38 years: "When Jesus saw him lying there and knew that he had been there a long time, he said to him, 'Do you want to be made well?' The sick man answered him, 'Sir, I have no one to put me into the pool when the water is stirred up; and while I am making my way, someone else steps down ahead of me.' Jesus said to him, 'Stand up, take your mat and walk.' At once the man was made well, and he took up his mat and began to walk. Now that day was a sabbath" (John 5:6–9).

Biblical scholars have long puzzled over the story of the healing at the Pool of Bethesda. For one thing, the pool found among the excavated ruins did not have "five porches" as stated in the biblical text. And how was it possible to lower people into the huge basins, nearly 50 feet deep?

Archaeologists solved the mystery in 1950. A pagan sanctuary, dedicated to the healing god Aesclepius, a minor but popular Greek god, was uncovered adjoining the Pool of Bethesda. The shrine dated to the time of Jesus and was identified by the unearthed image of a serpent coiled around a pole, the symbol of the Aesclepian Cult (analogous to the "caduceus," the physicians' symbol).

In each of the more than 200 Aesclepian shrines scattered throughout ancient Greece and Rome, the infirm would follow much the same ritual. After offering a sacrifice in a temple devoted to Aesclepius, they would immerse themselves in a ritual pool; then they would ingest a hallucinogenic substance and retire to a darkened, cavelike niche. The drug-induced dreams that would follow formed the basis for a priest's diagnosis.

At the Pool of Bethesda, these excavated underground chambers are clearly visible surrounding a small pool. This fits well with the details of the biblical text. The Aesclepian temple at the Pool of Bethesda also accounts for the reason a "great number of disabled people" were gathered there: The site had become a healing shrine.

Not Even in Israel

 n the Gospel of Luke, we read that Jesus was approached by the Jewish elders of Capernaum as he was entering the city. They came to ask him to heal the servant of a Roman officer, or "centurion." To our twentieth-century minds, this may not seem unusual, but given the political tensions of the day, it was an extraordinary request. The Jews hated the Roman occupiers of their country with a passion. That hatred later resulted in two ferocious revolts that would level the country and destroy the Jewish nation.

So why did the Jewish elders come to Jesus on behalf of a Roman military commander? The answer to this question is given in their own words: "This man deserves to have you do this, because he loves our nation and has built our synagogue" (Luke 7:4–5).

The visitor to Capernaum today can view an imposing structure of white limestone that stands in the midst of the black

basalt buildings of the ancient town. This synagogue, dated to
the fourth century, is built over the original synagogue to which
the elders were referring.

Visitors can explore the nearby fields where, hidden in the
overgrowth, the partially excavated remains of a Roman military
camp can be found. Recent excavations have uncovered a Roman-
style bathhouse and other large, well-constructed buildings.

This is where the centurion's sick servant lay. Jesus went with
the elders to the camp to visit him. However, "the centurion sent
friends to say to him, 'Lord, do not trouble yourself, for I am not
worthy to have you come under my roof; therefore I did not pre-
sume to come to you. But only speak the word, and let my servant be healed.' . . . When Jesus heard this he was amazed at him,
and turning to the crowd that followed him, he said, 'I tell you,
not even in Israel have I found such faith.' When those who had
been sent returned to the house, they found the slave in good
health" (Luke 7:6–7, 9–10).

Was Lazarus Raised
from Death?

n chapter 11 of the Gospel of John, we read that "a
certain man was ill, Lazarus of Bethany, the village
of Mary and her sister Martha" (John 11:1). Jesus was
in the wilderness of the Jordan River when he was told of his
friend's sickness. He did not leave immediately, although

Jesus raising Lazarus from the tomb.

Bethany would have been perhaps a day's journey away.

It is only after Lazarus dies that Jesus goes to Bethany. In a foreshadowing of the miracle he would perform, he tells his disciples: "For your sake I am glad I was not there, so that you may believe. But let us go to him" (John 11:15). If Jesus had arrived when Lazarus was still alive, the miracle would have been one of healing. Instead, an even greater miracle was performed in Bethany.

It is significant that Jesus delayed three days, arriving on the fourth. According to Jewish custom, the spirit of the dead person hovers over the body for three days before departing. This tradition may have arisen because of instances when those who appeared to be dead, but were actually comatose, revived later in the tomb. By waiting three days, Jesus was undermining those who might claim that Lazarus was never truly dead.

When Jesus approached the tomb, "he cried with a loud voice, 'Lazarus, come out!' The dead man came out, his hands and feet bound with strips of cloth, and his face wrapped in a cloth. Jesus said to them, 'Unbind him, and let him go'" (John 11:44). Some speculate that Jesus was careful to specify Lazarus' name when he commanded him to come forth. If he had not, then all the dead would have arisen.

The Arab village of al-Azariyeh, several miles east of Jerusalem, marks the site of Bethany. The name reflects the Greek "Lazarion," meaning "the place of Lazarus." Archaeological excavation here has discovered a cemetery dating from the first century, and in the fourth century a church was built over a specific rock-cut chamber thought to belong to Lazarus. The tomb, as it was after Jesus raised Lazarus, remains empty.

The Notorious Pontius Pilate

p until A.D. 6, Palestine had been in the firm control of Herod the Great, followed by his son Archelaus, who succeeded him. After Archelaus was deposed, Rome was concerned about the security of the land bridge between Africa and Asia. To keep the rebellious population in check, Rome annexed Judea as a province and governed it through a series of praefects, or governors.

The fifth of these was Pontius Pilate, who ruled from A.D. 26 to 36. He came to power at a time when Jews were being persecuted both in Rome and in the adjoining province of Egypt. Pilate wasted no time in taking up the same harsh tactics, and his actions led to a confrontation shortly after he took office.

Wherever Rome ruled, images of Caesar, known as standards, were displayed in military camps and headquarters. These standards, however, greatly offended the Jews, who believed

An Inscription to Pilate

In 1961, the only known inscription mentioning Pontius Pilate was found among the ruins of Caesarea Maritima along the Mediterranean coast of northern Israel. It happened while an Italian archaeological team was excavating the theater, which was dated to the third and fourth century A.D.

Builders in ancient Israel used materials from ruined structures whenever possible. Since most buildings were constructed from stone, this saved the trouble of quarrying new blocks. It was one of these recycled blocks that gave us Pilate's inscription. When archaeologists were examining the seats of the theater, they turned one of the stone blocks over and found the following inscription in Greek: "Pontius Pilate, Praefect of Judea, made and dedicated the Tiberium to the Divine Augustus."

The word "praefect" (*praefectus*) is the Latin word for governor. A "Tiberium" is a temple or shrine honoring the Roman emperor Tiberius Claudius Caesar Augustus. The temple mentioned in the inscription has not been found.

that any such image worship constituted idolatry. Pilate's predecessors had respected the Jewish sensibilities and did not bring the standards up to Jerusalem.

Josephus relates how Pilate, intent upon demonstrating his authority, had the standards secretly brought to Jerusalem under cover of darkness. When the Jews discovered the standards the next morning, the city erupted into riots. A huge mob rushed to Pilate's headquarters in Caesarea and demanded that the standards be removed. When he refused, the crowd staged a giant sit-in around his residence.

The next day, Pilate summoned the crowd to the stadium, where he had them surrounded by soldiers and threatened with death unless they ceased their protests. At his nod, the soldiers drew their swords to show he meant business. To Pilate's amazement, instead of yielding to his ultimatum, the Jews fell to the ground and bared their necks, saying they preferred to die rather than see their law trampled on.

The Jews won that round. Pilate ordered the standards to be removed from Jerusalem. But there would be other tests of will between Pilate and his unwilling subjects.

Josephus records that Pilate stirred up further trouble by taking funds from the Temple treasury to build an aqueduct. This time when the Jews protested, he was better prepared. He had his soldiers dress in civilian clothing and mix with the crowd that gathered outside his residence in Jerusalem. When he gave the signal, they took out their weapons and killed many of the protesters.

Each of the four Gospels has numerous references to Pontius Pilate and his role in the trial and crucifixion of Jesus. It is surprising, given his dislike for the Jews, that Pilate agreed with their demand that Jesus be put to death.

Jesus before Pontius Pilate.

The Gospels record his uncertainty: "You brought me this man as one who was perverting the people; and here I have examined him in your presence and have not found this man guilty of any of your charges against him" (Luke 23:14).

The date of Jesus' crucifixion is not certain, but Pilate ruled for several more years until another crisis brought his rule to an end. This time he cruelly attacked a group of Samaritan worshipers who had gathered on Mount Gerizim, supposing them to be preparing a revolt. The Samaritans complained to Pilate's immediate superior, Vitellius, governer of Syria, and Pilate was ordered to give an account in Rome. Few mourned his leaving, and he soon disappeared from history.

The Secret of the Cross

 rucifixion was a brutal form of capital punishment used by the Romans as a deterrent against the most serious crimes and to keep rebellious provinces in check. The Jewish historian Josephus called it the "most wretched of deaths."

Illustrations of Jesus carrying a square-cut cross to Golgotha are probably incorrect. While there were several varieties of crosses on which the victims were hung, in most cases the condemned carried only the crossbar, the center post was often the trunk of a tree.

Wood being scarce in Jerusalem, both the tree and the crossbar were probably reused. [Josephus records that during the siege of Jerusalem in A.D. 70, the Romans were forced to gather wood from ten miles away for their siege machinery.]

A highly visible site was chosen for crucifixions to make an example of the victim. In Jerusalem of Jesus' day, one such site was called Golgotha, meaning "the place of a skull." The Gospels indicate that Jesus was put to death along a highway, for we read that, "Those who passed by derided him, shaking their heads" (Matthew 27:39).

Sentences were typically carried out immediately after being pronounced. Upon arriving at the site of crucifixion, the condemned was stripped, flogged, then placed on the ground and roped or nailed to the crossbar, which was then lifted into place on the center post.

One feature of the cross reveals the true cruelty of crucifixion. There was a small wooden block or "seat" placed beneath the buttocks to support the weight of the torso. This was not to provide comfort for the victim, but to prolong the agony. To breathe, the condemned man had to push himself up on his nailed feet, causing terrible pain.

Death on the cross resulted from asphyxiation due to the weakening of the diaphragm and the chest muscles. The Romans had evidently learned from much experience that the doomed died too quickly to suit their purposes. However, the crucified person would often hang on the cross for days, expiring slowly from a combination of dehydration, exposure to the elements, and the effects of the scourging.

We read that "they offered him [Jesus] wine to drink, mixed with gall; but when he tasted it, he would not drink it" (Matthew 27:34). The meaning of "gall" is uncertain. Some equate it with the hemlock poison that Socrates drank. If so, it was an offer

The Crucified Man

There are nine references to crucifixion in the works of Josephus, but until 1968, no physical specimen of a crucified man was known to exist. In that year, a burial tomb excavated at Givat HaMivtar, north of Jerusalem, was found to contain the skeletons of a young man and woman.

When the young man was examined, he was found to have a four-and-a-half inch iron spike through his left heelbone, indicating he had been crucified. The nail was not removed before burial because the tip was bent, apparently from hitting a knot in the cross, making removal difficult. According to Jewish custom, the dead had to be buried before sunset, and there may not have been time to remove it.

A block of wood was attached to the head of the nail, probably to prevent it from being wrenched out by the victim. From this evidence, scholars have sketched what the crucifixion of the man from Givat HaMivtar probably looked like. His feet were likely nailed on either side of the upright post. The man's fingers and wrists gave no sign of traumatic injury, thus indicating that his arms were tied to the cross rather than nailed.

The legs of the man from Givat HaMivtar were not broken before he expired. When it was convenient for death to be hastened, the soldiers would break the legs of the condemned man. This made it impossible for the man to push up and gasp for breath, and he would suffocate more quickly. However, the Gospel of John records that "when they came to Jesus and saw that he was already dead, they did not break his legs" (John 19:33).

to Jesus to help put an end to his suffering, which he refused. Others suggest the liquid may have contained opium, given to him according to Jewish custom.

The Romans put a placard around the neck of the condemned man on which his offense was written. According to the Gospels, Pilate had an inscription put on the cross that read: "Jesus of Nazareth, the King of the Jews."

The Jews, however, objected to Pilate's choice of words, because it seemed to confirm what they had so strenuously denied: "Then the chief priests of the Jews said to Pilate, 'Do not write, "The King of the Jews," but, "This man said, I am King of the Jews."' Pilate answered, 'What I have written I have written'" (John 19:19, 21–22).

Where Is the Tomb of Christ?

here are two main possibilities in Jerusalem for the site of the crucifixion, burial, and resurrection of Christ. The first is the Garden Tomb, which was discovered by the British General Charles Gordon in 1883 while he was visiting Jerusalem. General Gordon noticed caves in the side of a hill just outside the walls of Jerusalem that gave the visual impression of the eye sockets of a skull. He deduced that this hill was Golgotha, where Jesus was crucified, since "Golgotha" means "skull."

Subsequent excavation of the area revealed a tomb cut into the same hill. Above the tomb was what appeared to be the sign of the cross. Nearby was a large cistern that some believed was used to water an ancient garden at the site. The Gospel of John mentions that Mary mistook Jesus for a gardener, suggesting the tomb was in a garden.

However, the tomb itself is the same age as an Iron Age tomb complex located on the property of St. Stephen's Church next door. This means that the Garden Tomb was carved hundreds of years before the time of Christ and could hardly qualify as the "new tomb" of Joseph of Arimathea. (The Iron Age extended in Palestine, circa 1200–586 B.C.)

Scores of tombs have been found outside the walls of Jerusalem, as well as dozens of Byzantine monastic sites. It is probable that the Garden Tomb was the site of a monastery in the centuries after Christ and that the tomb was reused for Christian burial.

The other possible site for the crucifixion, burial, and resurrection of Christ is that of the historic Church of the Holy Sepulcher. Although the church is inside the present-day walls of Jerusalem, it was outside the walls of the city that existed in the days of Jesus.

Archaeological soundings inside the Church have confirmed that the site was used as a quarry until the first century B.C., when it was filled in and used as a garden or orchard. Several tombs dating from the first century A.D. confirm that the area was used as a cemetery in the time of Jesus.

The Roman Emperor Hadrian contributed unwittingly to the preservation of the site of Jesus' death and resurrection. After his legions suppressed the Second Jewish Revolt of A.D. 132–135, Hadrian determined to put an end to any further revolt. He banned Jews from the destroyed Jerusalem and rebuilt it as a Roman City, which he named Aelia Capitolina. He also changed the name of the country from Judea to Palaestina, or Palestine.

Hadrian attempted to remove all places of Jewish and Christian worship in Jerusalem. One of these, which the early Christians revered as the tomb of Christ, was covered with a massive

The Bones of Caiaphas' Family Discovered

The Gospels record that on the night of Jesus' arrest he was taken to "Caiaphas the high priest, in whose house the scribes and the elders had gathered" (Matthew 26:57).

During a mockery of a trial in which various false witnesses were introduced but failed to collaborate their stories, Caiaphas asked Jesus directly whether he was the Messiah: "Jesus said to him, 'You have said so. But I tell you, from now on you will see the Son of Man seated at the right hand of Power and coming on the clouds of heaven.' Then the high priest tore his clothes and said, 'He has blasphemed! Why do we still need witnesses? You have now heard his blasphemy. What is your verdict?' They answered, 'He deserves death.'" (Matthew 26:64–66).

Thus the Gospels indicate that Caiaphas was a leader in the plot to have Jesus put to death. Little is known of him outside the New Testament, other than that he apparently served as high priest from about A.D. 18 to A.D. 36.

In 1990, workers building a water park outside the Old City of Jerusalem broke into an ancient burial cave dating from the first century A.D. Inside were the remains of 12 "ossuaries," ornately carved limestone containers that served as secondary repositories for bones. In the first century, it was common Jewish custom to deposit the body in a tomb until the flesh decayed, after which the bones were collected and put into an ossuary.

Numerous ossuaries have been found in the Jerusalem area. However, this particular discovery caused a sensation when two of the accompanying inscriptions included the name Caiaphas. The full text of one of the inscriptions was deciphered to read: "Joseph, Son of Caiaphas." This marked the first archaeological confirmation of the existence of the high priest who was instrumental in having Jesus condemned to death.

platform and a temple to Venus. Ironically, in attempting to obliterate the Christian holy place, he permanently marked the site of Calvary under the temple. Less than 200 years later, Constantine the Great converted to Christianity and wasted no time in commissioning the bishop Macarius to build a basilica commemorating the death and resurrection of Christ.

There was little doubt in anyone's mind where the actual location was. Even though the church could have been built in an open area nearby, Constantine insisted that it be built upon the exact site. Accordingly, the pagan temple was destroyed and underneath was found the tomb believed to be that of Jesus. The basilica erected over that tomb is known today, after considerable alterations through the centuries, as the Church of the Holy Sepulcher.

A Controversial Passage From Josephus

 mong the references made by ancient writers regarding Jesus of Nazareth, none is more remarkable—and controversial—than that recorded by Josephus in his *History of the Jews*:

"About this time there lived Jesus, a wise man, if indeed one ought to call him a man. For he was one who wrought surprising feats and was a teacher of such people as accept the truth gladly. He won over many Jews and many of the Greeks. He was the Messiah. When Pilate, upon hearing him accused by men of the highest standing amongst us, had condemned him to be crucified, those who had in the first place come to love him did not give up their affection for him. On the third day he appeared to them restored to life, for the prophets of God had prophesied these and countless other marvelous things about him. And the tribe of the Christians, so called after him, has still to this day not disappeared" (18:63–64).

This passage, known as Josephus' "Testimonium," appears to be an astounding testimony to Jesus being the Messiah—and of his resurrection—by a non-Christian ancient source. To some, it would have been unthinkable for a Jewish historian to make such an admission. Therefore it has been suggested that the passage must have been altered at a later date to include the distinctly Christian elements. As Josephus' works

Josephus, the Jewish historian.

were preserved and handed down by the Church, there would have been ample opportunity for the texts to be secretly revised.

One thing is certain. The Testimonium cannot be dismissed as a late fabrication. The text is quoted in its entirety by the fourth-century Church historian Eusebius in his *History of the Church*. Eusebius was a meticulous historian, who thoroughly researched his sources. Despite his obvious enthusiasm for defending and furthering the Gospel, there is no evidence he willfully used fraudulent source material to prove his point.

It is then left for some unknown Christian scribe in the time before Eusebius to have supposedly altered the text to include what he believed to be some critical details about the life of Christ. But this assumes a willingness to engage in and condone an obvious fraud on the part of those in the early Church, which runs contrary to the fundamental moral axioms of their faith. The church did not depend upon secular historians for proof of their most important doctrines, and it is difficult to fathom the purpose in attempting to put words in Josephus' mouth.

Unfortunately, as no other ancient manuscript versions of the passage are available for comparison, a definitive answer to the controversy over Josephus' Testimonium may never be forthcoming. But even if the disputed references to the Messiah and the resurrection are found to be a later inclusion, all is not lost: The passage remains a valuable confirmation by an extra-biblical source of the historical existence of Jesus Christ.

The Authenticity of the Shroud of Turin

 cholars and the faithful alike have been fascinated by a mysterious artifact called the Shroud of Turin, which some claim to be the burial shroud of Jesus. After more than two decades of careful investigation and scientific analysis, there still is no consensus as to the shroud's authenticity.

The Shroud of Turin has a long and colorful history. It has been suggested that the shroud is the same cloth as the sixth-century *mandylion,* or face cloth, of Edessa (modern Urfa, in Turkey). The image of Christ was also allegedly displayed on the *mandylion,* which was brought to Constantinople in the tenth century. The *mandylion* remained in Constantinople as late as the thirteenth century, after which it disappeared from history. Some believe it was transferred to Europe, where it eventually became known as the Shroud of Turin.

The cloth known as the Shroud of Turin appeared in 1357, when it was exhibited in the village of Lirey in northern France. In 1460, the shroud passed into the hands of the House of Savoy, which held legal title to it until 1983. The shroud was partially burned in 1532, when fire swept through the chapel in the castle at Chambery, where it was kept in a silver chest. The image, however, was largely undamaged.

Approximately 45 years later, the shroud was brought to the city of Turin in northern Italy, where it resides today in the Royal Chapel of the Cathedral of St. John. The chest in which it is held requires three different keys to open, and the shroud is exhibited only on rare occasions—nine times in the past two centuries. On the four hundredth anniversary of the shroud's arrival in Turin, it was viewed by more than three million people over a six-week period.

Even though the shroud was exhibited frequently during the late medieval and Renaissance periods, it was never officially proclaimed by the Church to be Jesus' actual burial cloth. To the contrary, a number of Church pronouncements through the centuries exhibited caution regarding the origin of the shroud.

The first scientific indication of the unusual nature of the shroud came in 1898, when it was photographed with glass-plate negatives. It was discovered that the image on the plate was a positive, an anomaly that, if faked, was produced hundreds of years before the invention of photography.

In 1973, a group of European scientists was permitted to inspect the shroud in order to recommend how best to preserve it. Upon examining the shroud, the scientists were divided in their opinions concerning its authenticity.

A year later, two U.S. Air Force scientists processed some photographs of the shroud with a computer image analyzer used to transform satellite photographs into three-dimensional topographical reliefs. To the scientists' surprise, a relatively undistorted three-dimensional image was produced by the analyzer. This would have been impossible if the image on the shroud had been painted on the fabric.

This was the beginning of the Shroud of Turin Research Project (STURP), involving more than 30 researchers from various highly respected scientific institutions in the United States. In their religious beliefs, the scientists varied from confirmed believers to agnostics.

The first problem that the STURP team tackled was the alleged bloodstains on the shroud. In 1973, Italian specialists were unable to confirm that the stains were blood. However, after running a series of sophisticated experiments, two experts on the

STURP team concluded that the stains were in fact made by blood.

Some continued to disagree, claiming that the alleged bloodstains are from iron-oxide pigment painted on the linen. The iron-oxide theory, however, to date, has not been verified by scientific analysis.

It has also been pointed out that the bright-red color of the bloodstains suggests they are of relatively recent origin. Others, however, point out that the shroud may have been washed with soapwart, a plant used as a detergent in antiquity. Soapwart has a preserving effect upon blood cells.

Other evidence appears to tie the shroud to the land of Israel. Scientists removed pollen spores embedded in the shroud that are native to the area of the Dead Sea and other parts of Palestine.

In the 1980s, investigators also found calcium carbonate (limestone) particles on the shroud. Microscopic examination revealed that the particular type of limestone was not the more common calcite, but travertine argonite deposited from springs.

Argonite is also the type of limestone common to the hill country of Judea, so investigators decided to obtain limestone samples from ancient tombs in Jerusalem. Both the limestone particles on the shroud and the samples from Jerusalem tombs were tested by a device called a high-resolution scanning ion microprobe.

The graphs produced by the microprobe revealed that the samples were an unusually close match, indicating that the shroud had at one time been in a Jerusalem tomb. This positive evidence was seemingly overturned in 1988, when the Vatican permitted a few pieces of thread from the shroud to be tested by a method of carbon–14 dating using accelerated mass spectrometry. Three laboratories, working independently, arrived at a date of origin between 1260 and 1390. These findings seemed to confirm the theory that the shroud was created around 1350 by Geoffrey de Charny, a French knight who hoped to attract pilgrims to his newly built church.

The mystery of the shroud continued, however, as other researchers pointed out that the image itself contains extraordinarily precise physical details that only the most accomplished medieval artist could have hoped to attain. However, there are no brush strokes or pigments visible on the surface of the shroud indicating that the linen was not painted.

In addition, the carbon–14 dating of the shroud has been challenged on the basis of new research. Scientists have discovered that various microbes can cover ancient artifacts with plasticlike coatings that significantly alter the results of carbon–14 analysis. That, combined with the minuscule amount of fabric tested, increased the possibility that the initial carbon–14 test results were invalid.

What seems clear is that the image of a man estimated to be just under six feet tall, weighing 175 pounds, and between the ages of 30 and 35 has been inexplicably imprinted on the surface of the fabric. While the faithful and the skeptics continue to disagree concerning whose image it may be, it is hoped that further investigation will someday establish with more certainty the date—and authenticity—of the Shroud of Turin.

The Indestructible Temple Mount

n Mount Moriah in Jerusalem stands one of the most imposing structures of the ancient world. It is a massive structure called the Temple Mount. Towering above the Kidron Valley, it covers a quarter of the area of the ancient city.

The Temple that Jesus knew was called the Second Temple. The first—Solomon's—was destroyed in 586 B.C. by the Babylonians. In 520 B.C., under Zerubbabel, the Temple was rebuilt on a modest scale. This structure was used until the time of Herod the Great.

Herod decided to construct an edifice that would be as much of a lasting tribute to himself as it was to the God of his Jewish subjects. Not content to rebuild Zerubbabel's temple, the temple that Herod began in 20 B.C. doubled its area. At a size of 24 football fields, the Temple Mount was the largest artificial platform in the ancient world. Such a massive structure required the kind of technical innovation at which the Romans excelled. The lower end of the platform, for example, could not merely be filled in with rubble lest the walls burst out from the pressure. To solve the problem, the southern end of the Temple Mount was built upon huge vaulted structures known traditionally—but erroneously—as "Solomon's Stables."

As prophesied by Jesus, the Temple itself was destroyed by the Romans in A.D. 70. The Temple Mount was ploughed and a temple to Jupiter was built upon the site. That structure is long gone, and the Temple Mount is now dominated by the Muslim al-Aksa mosque and the Dome of the Rock shrine.

The immense foundation and retaining wall of the Jewish Temple, however, have withstood the ravages of time and continue to dominate the vista of the Old City. Tour guides point out the colossal limestone blocks, some of which are 40 feet in length and weigh as many tons. They were joined so masterfully—without cement—that not even a piece of paper could be slipped between the blocks.

Engineering Feats of the First Century

he Temple that Herod built for the Jewish people was one of the most impressive buildings of ancient times. Even today, the visitor to Jerusalem can see the enormous blocks used in its massive retaining wall.

The Jews were hesitant to permit Herod to dismantle the modest temple that Zerubbabel had rebuilt hundreds of years earlier. What if he razed the building and then went back on his promise to build the new temple? Only after Herod promised to have all of the materials prepared for the new temple did they agree to have the old structure dismantled.

As part of his preparations, Herod employed ten thousand workers, including a thousand priests who were trained as masons.

The priests were necessary to build the inner temple, to which only priests were allowed access.

The stone used to construct the Temple came from quarries around Jerusalem, some of which can still be seen. The stone was freed from the rock by hammering wooden beams into chiseled grooves. The pressure was sufficient to break the rock free. The next step was squaring off the stones to specific dimensions, after which the smaller blocks were placed on wagons and transported to the Temple site.

The larger blocks, weighing many tons, could not be placed on carts. Herod's Roman engineers solved the problem by developing special techniques to move them. The stones were placed on special rollers and then pulled to the site. According to Josephus, at least one thousand oxen were used to complete the task. The known quarries were at a higher elevation than the Temple site, and using gravity made moving the stones easier.

Once the stones arrived, they had to be put into position—no mean feat, considering that stones weighing 80 tons were positioned at least 100 feet above the foundations. To lift stones of that size was beyond the capability of the most sophisticated engineering equipment of the day.

Scholars believe that, as the 16-foot-wide walls were laid course by course, each successive layer became the construction platform for the next. The blocks for each course would arrive from the higher elevation at the northern end of the site and were moved down to their position.

The surviving retaining wall is 40 courses high, or the height of a 15-story building. It was originally significantly higher. The project took decades to complete. Herod began building around 20 B.C., and the main construction was done by Jesus' day. However, it was not until A.D. 64 that the temple was finally completed and dedicated.

All the effort made to create what the historian Josephus calls "the most wonderful edifice ever seen or heard" would soon come to naught. In A.D. 70, only six years after being dedicated, the great Jewish temple was completely destroyed by the conquering Romans.

The Fall of Jerusalem

uring the final week before his crucifixion, Jesus was coming out of the Temple with his disciples when they pointed out to him the magnificence of the structure. They were no doubt shocked by his reply: "You see all these, do you not? Truly I tell you, not one stone will be left here upon another; all will be thrown down" (Matthew 24:2).

The Gospel of Luke includes more of what Jesus had to say about the destruction of the Temple: "When you see Jerusalem surrounded by armies, then know that its desolation has come near. Woe to those who are pregnant and to those who are nursing infants in those days! For there will be great distress on the earth and wrath against this people; they will fall by the edge of the sword and be taken away as captives among all nations; and Jerusalem will be trampled on by the Gentiles, until the times of the Gentiles are fulfilled" (Luke 21:20, 23, 24).

Vespasian and his son Titus.

The Jewish historian Josephus, who witnessed the fall of Jerusalem that Jesus foretold, describes the siege in horrendous detail. In the spring of A.D. 70, an enormous army commanded by Titus, totaling almost 80,000 men, set up camp around Jerusalem.

The city was swarming with refugees and pilgrims who, despite the war, had come to celebrate Passover. All pleas to surrender were rebuffed by the inhabitants, who had supreme confidence in the city's defenses. On the south, Jerusalem was protected by steep cliffs, and on the more vulnerable north side, a series of three massive walls stood between the defenders and the Romans.

Titus gave the order to attack. The Roman artillery included siege engines that battered the walls and stone throwers that could hurl hundred-pound rocks as far as 600 feet.

To the dismay of the defenders, it took just two weeks for the Roman siege machines to break through the outermost northern wall. In another five days, the second wall was breached. Titus was sure the city would surrender, but its inhabitants spurned his attempts to get them to do so. Sending Josephus to plead with his former compatriots met with no success.

The battle began anew. All Judeans caught outside the city were summarily executed. Hundreds were nailed to crosses in full view of their comrades within the city. The practice was halted only when there were no more trees left.

Inside the city, food became scarce. Josephus records that the hunger of the Jerusalemites became so great that they ate old hay and chewed their belts and shoes. Many died of starvation, but there was no place to bury the dead, so the bodies had to be thrown over the walls. Soon, thousands of corpses lay rotting along the town's perimeter.

The Romans finally succeeded in breaking through to the Temple, which was soon set ablaze. From there, they swept down into the rest of the city and began a horrible slaughter. Of the estimated 600,000 men, women, and children in Jerusalem at the beginning of the siege, only 97,000 prisoners were accounted for.

To ensure that Judea would not rise up again, the tenth Roman legion was stationed in the city for the next 60 years. Nevertheless, the flames of revolt would be stirred up once more in A.D. 135 with the Bar Kochba Revolt, which brought even more devastating consequences.

How the Temple Walls Came Tumbling Down

While in Jerusalem during the last week before his crucifixion, Jesus was approached by one of his followers, who was impressed by Herod's building achievements: "As he came out of the temple, one of his disciples said to him, 'Look, Teacher, what large stones and what large buildings!' Then Jesus asked him, 'Do you see these great buildings? Not one stone will be left here upon another; all will be thrown down'" (Mark 13:1–2).

Jesus' prophecy was fulfilled in A.D. 70 when a Roman legion under Titus conquered Jerusalem, thus ending the First Jewish Revolt. Knowing the proportions of Herod's Temple, scholars have puzzled over how such a massive stone structure could have been completely destroyed.

Although most of the building materials of the Temple have long disappeared, much of the massive retaining wall can still be seen today. This wall holds the secrets of what happened to the structure above it.

The stones of the retaining wall of the Temple are beautifully trimmed with beveled edges. The outside face was joined so perfectly without mortar of any kind that even today a piece of paper cannot fit between many of the joints. The engineers, realizing that limestone expands as its moisture content increases, carefully left space behind the surface of the blocks to allow for expansion.

Normally, the expansion and contraction occurs without harming the rock. However, when the Romans took Jerusalem, overzealous soldiers set fire to the Temple, against the orders of their commander, Titus.

It was this fire that spelled the doom of the building. As the limestone was rapidly heated, the moisture in the rock could not escape quickly enough. The result was that the superheated moisture caused the blocks to explode, collapsing the walls of the Temple. Only the retaining wall below survived the conflagration.

The Apostles
How Did Judas Die?

n the Gospel of Matthew, we read that, after betraying Jesus, Judas repented. He went back to the Jewish authorities and attempted to return the 30 pieces of silver they paid him to lead the way to Jesus: "He said, 'I have sinned by betraying innocent blood.' But they said, 'What is that to us? See to it yourself'" (Matthew 27:4).

The temple officials refused to take the money back because it was considered "blood money" and therefore unsuitable for an offering to God. Judas then threw down the pieces of silver in the Temple and "went and hanged himself" (Matthew 27:5).

The Book of Acts, however, gives a different account of how Judas died. The Apostle Peter reminds the disciples of the circumstances of Jesus' betrayal and states how Judas died: "Now this man acquired a field with the reward of his wickedness; and falling headlong, he burst open in the middle and all his bowels gushed out. This became known to all the residents of Jerusalem, so that the field was called in their language Akeldama, that is, Field of Blood" (Acts 1:18–19).

How, then, did Judas die—by hanging, or because of his fall? An examination of the probable area where his death occurred shows that he may have suffered both of those calamities.

One might be tempted to picture Judas hanging from gallows, such as those pictured in Western films. But such a contraption would have been unknown in ancient Israel. Indeed, hanging was not used as a form of execution, although the

corpses of those put to death by stoning or the sword were sometimes hung afterward from a convenient tree.

Both the historian Eusebius and the early church father
Jerome mention that the site of Judas' hanging was known in their
day (circa A.D. 330). We can expect that the early Christians in
Jerusalem would have remembered the site, and, together with
the location of other significant events, passed this knowledge
along to succeeding gener-
ations.

Judas Iscariot and his bag of silver.

The site of Akeldama
has been preserved
through the centuries by
the Monastery of St.
Onuphrius, on a steep hill-
side in the Hinnom Valley
outside the walls of the
Old City of Jerusalem.
Today, gnarled olive trees
dot the steep hillsides and
cliffs of the Hinnom. One
might expect Judas to
come to a place such as
this outside the city walls
to hang himself.

It is easy to picture
what might have happened. After tying the rope to a branch of
a tree overlooking the Hinnom, Judas would have jumped to his
death. If the rope did not hold, his body would have hurtled down

the cliff and been disemboweled, perhaps by a sharp rock or some other obstruction below.

Was it God or the Luck of the Draw?

n the first chapter of Acts, we read the account of how the disciples chose a replacement for Judas: "And they cast lots for them, and the lot fell on Matthias; and he was added to the eleven apostles" (Acts 1:26).

Lots are mentioned throughout Scripture for determining Divine will. Proverbs 16:33 states: "The lot is cast into the lap, but the decision is the Lord's alone." The division of the Promised Land among the 12 tribes of Israel was determined by choosing lots, as was the Temple priests' order of service.

The Urim and Thummim were a similar means used by the priests to inquire of the Lord. Nowhere in Scripture are the objects themselves or their exact method of use described. One suggestion is that they were shaped stones inscribed with symbols that were put into a vessel, then shaken until one jumped out, or perhaps they were drawn from a bag.

Saul used Urim and Thummim to determine who had broken his vow in a battle with the Philistines: "Then Saul said, 'O Lord God of Israel, why have you not answered your servant today? If this guilt is in me or in my son Jonathan, O Lord God of Israel, give Urim; but if this guilt is in your people Israel, give

Thummim.' And Jonathan and Saul were indicated by the lot, but the people were cleared. Then Saul said, 'Cast the lot between me and my son Jonathan.' And Jonathan was taken" (1 Samuel 14:41–42).

This text suggests that the Urim and Thummim each represented one possible answer to the question being asked of the Lord. Saul used a series of castings of the Urim and Thummim to pinpoint the guilty party.

The Book of Joshua relates how Achan, son of Zerah, hid stolen booty in his tent, which was the cause of the initial defeat of the Israelites when they attacked the city of Ai. Although lots are not specifically mentioned as being used by Joshua to determine the guilt of Achan, the method is similar: "So Joshua rose early in the morning, and brought Israel near tribe by tribe, and the tribe of Judah was taken. He brought near the clans of Judah, and the clan of the Zerahites was taken; and he brought near the clan of the Zerahites, family by family, and Zabdi was taken. And he brought near his household one by one, and Achan son of Carmi... was taken" (Joshua 7:16–18). In the book of Jonah, the Phoenician sailors used the lot to single out Jonah as the cause of their distress in the storm, a fact he did not dispute (Jonah 1:7–12). The accuracy of the lot was well accepted.

To the Western mind, the use of lots may seem like reliance on blind chance. Not so to the ancients, who believed God revealed his will through such means. In fact, the use of lots was preferable to making a decision through reasoning, because it removed the possibility of human error in determining the will of God.

Why Did Joseph Move to Galilee?

fter the birth of Jesus, his family fled to Egypt, having been warned in a dream that Herod the Great was about to search for them. After Herod died, Joseph was told in another dream to return to Israel: "Then Joseph got up, took the child and his mother, and went to the land of Israel. However, when Joseph heard that Archelaus was ruling over Judea in place of his father Herod, he was afraid to go there. And after being warned in a dream, he went away to the district of Galilee" (Matthew 2:21–22).

Other ancient historical sources shed light upon why Joseph avoided returning to Judea. The story begins ten years earlier when Archelaus began his tumultuous ten-year reign in Judea. Archelaus was no more accepted by the Jews than was Herod the Great, and after a brief attempt to win them over, he resorted to harsh tactics that exceeded those of his father.

Not long after the beginning of his reign, Archelaus suppressed a mob protest by force, killing 3,000 people in Jerusalem. Tensions grew as representatives from the elders were sent to Rome to demand that Archelaus be removed.

As Archelaus went to appear before Caesar to defend himself against his accusers, violence erupted back home in Judea. It was the time of the feast of Passover, and an enormous crowd gathered in Jerusalem—not to celebrate the feast, but to seize control of the city in protest of Archelaus' rule.

As revolt spread across the land, Quintilius Varus, the Roman legate of Syria, came swiftly with three powerful legions to restore order. After a series of pitched battles, Judea was again subdued. In retribution, Varus crucified 2,000 of the rebels. These events were taking place when Joseph was returning from Egypt. He wisely decided to skirt the troubles in Judea, settling in the Galilean village of Nazareth.

Death in the Theater

Herod Agrippa I, the grandson of Herod the Great, ruled over Judea between A.D. 41 and 44. He maintained good relations with the Jews, but persecuted Christians. Agrippa was responsible for the beheading of James, the son of Zebedee, and for the imprisonment of the Apostle Peter.

Agrippa's sudden and unexpected end came at Caesarea. The Book of Acts tells us that his followers thought him a god. "On an appointed day Herod put on his royal robes, took his seat on the platform, and delivered a public address to them. The people kept shouting, 'The voice of a god, and not of a mortal!' And immediately, because he had not given the glory to God, an angel of the Lord struck him down, and he was eaten by worms and died" (Acts 12:21–23).

Imagine the dramatic scene. Agrippa, dressed in a glittering robe decorated with pieces of bright gold, stood with his back to the sea. The sun rising over the top of the theater cast his robe in a brilliant light. Hence the cry of the people as he addressed the crowd: "The voice of a god, and not of a mortal!" (Acts 12:22).

In some cultures, to be held up as a god was not uncommon for monarchs, but for pious Jews it was blasphemous. Josephus, author of *History of the Jews*, was in Caesarea to preside over games held in honor of the emperor. In his book, Josephus describes the final scene of Agrippa's life in detail. The Book of Acts states that he was "eaten by worms and died." In *History of the Jews*, Josephus says Agrippa died shortly afterward from an unknown intestinal disease.

Archelaus survived this test of his authority, but continued to exercise brutality toward his opponents. In his ninth year, after further emissaries were sent to Rome to demand his removal, Archelaus was banished to Vienne in Gaul. Thus began the age of direct Roman rule in Judea.

What Happened to the Disciples?

After his resurrection, Jesus gave his disciples the mandate that countless of his followers have taken: "Go therefore and make disciples of all nations, baptizing them in the name of the Father and of the Son and of the Holy Spirit, and teaching them to obey everything that I have commanded you" (Matthew 28:19–20).

According to historical sources and tradition, this command was carried out with amazing speed as they preached the Gospel throughout the known world. While fulfilling their mission, many of the original disciples gave their lives for their faith.

Jesus foretold how Peter's life would end: "'Very truly, I tell you, when you were younger, you used to fasten your own belt and go wherever you wished. But when you grow old, you will stretch out your hands, and someone else will fasten a belt around you and take you where you do not wish to go'" (John 21:18–19).

The New Testament reveals that the final journeys of the Apostles Peter and Paul were to Rome, where they suffered imprisonment and death. In his first epistle, written from the Roman capital, Peter relates that he was "a witness of the sufferings of Christ, as well as one who shares in the glory to be revealed" (1 Peter 5:1).

Writing to Timothy, Paul reveals his thoughts about his coming martyrdom: "As for me, I am already being poured out as a libation, and the time of my departure has come. I have fought the good fight, I have finished the race, I have kept the faith. From

Peter refused to be crucified in the same manner as his Lord.

now on, there is reserved for me the crown of righteousness, which the Lord, the righteous judge, will give me on that day, and not only to me but also to all who have longed for his appearing" (2 Timothy 4:6–8).

The early Church father Eusebius confirms that Peter and Paul died at the hands of Nero around the time of the infamous fire in A.D. 64, which consumed much of the city. When Peter was told he was to be crucified, the same punishment as was given to Jesus, he said he was unworthy and asked to be crucified upside down. According to ancient sources mentioned by

St. John, gospel writer and beloved disciple.

Eusebius, the tombs of Peter and Paul were located on the Vatican hill, under what is now the Basilica of St. Peter's.

We learn from Polycarp of Smyrna, who knew the Apostle John, that the "beloved disciple" lived at Ephesus in Asia Minor until the time of the Emperor Trajan (98–117 A.D.). He is said to have continued being a witness for the Christian faith, teaching and, on one occasion, raising a man from the dead. The Church father Tertullian, who lived from the middle of the first century until well into the second, mentions that John was eventually taken to Rome and cast into a cauldron of boiling oil, only to escape without harm.

James, the son of Zebedee, was said to be the first martyred disciple; Herod Agrippa put him to death in A.D. 44. However, in other accounts from later sources, James is said to have made a trip to Spain, where he became the country's patron saint. The alleged place of his burial was a major pilgrimage site during the Middle Ages.

James, the brother of Jesus, remained in Jerusalem. Josephus states that he was stoned to death in A.D. 62. A source recorded by Eusebius claims that he was cast down from the pinnacle of the Temple—an estimated 140 feet in height. When he survived the fall, he was clubbed to death.

Other disciples went everywhere preaching the Gospel message. We know, for example, that Mark went to Alexandria and that Thaddeus went to Edessa, in what is now Turkey.

Perhaps the most intriguing story is the one told about Thomas. The apocryphal Acts of Thomas, written in the third century, claims that he evangelized as far as India, where he founded a church. He is alleged to have worked as a carpenter, performed miracles, and to have died a martyr's death. To this day, a unique group of Syrian Christians, known as the "Chris-

---

Nero's Madness Unleashed

The historian Eusebius gives the following account of how the Emperor Nero's madness was unleashed against the Christians of Rome:

"When Nero's power was now firmly established, he gave himself up to unholy practices and took up arms against the God of the universe. To describe the monster of depravity that he became lies outside the scope of this present work. Many writers have recorded the facts about him in minute detail, enabling anyone who wishes to get a complete picture of his perverse and extraordinary madness, which led him to the senseless destruction of innumerable lives.... All this left one crime still to be added to his account—he was the first of the emperors to be declared enemy of the worship of Almighty God.... So it came about that this man, the first to be heralded as a conspicuous fighter against God, was led on to murder the apostles. It is recorded that, in his reign, Paul was beheaded in Rome itself and that Peter was crucified, and the record is confirmed that the cemeteries there are still called by the names of Peter and Paul" (*History of the Church* II:25).

tians of St. Thomas," exist among a population that is 97 percent non-Christian. They live in Malabar, on the southwest coast
of India, and claim to be the descendants of those converted by
the apostle. Thomas is reportedly buried near Madras. Modern
scholars of Christian church history have confirmed this with a
high degree of probability.

God's Window of Opportunity

 or much of Rome's history, the *Pax Romana* (peace
of Rome) was more ideal than reality. Rome was
often threatened militarily, or plagued by political
unrest or unstable leaders. Rarely was there able leadership, efficient administration, and peace for any length of time. However,
one such time was the Julio-Claudian dynasties, extending from
before the birth of Christ to the end of the first century, encom-
passing the time of Jesus and the apostles. Jesus was born during the reign of Augustus Caesar (27 B.C.–A.D. 14). Augustus rose
to prominence during one of Rome's most tumultuous periods,
at the time of the civil wars that followed the assassination of
Julius Caesar in 44 B.C. Augustus, whose original name was
Octavian, gained control over the West while his rival Anthony
ruled the East from Alexandria. In 31 B.C., their armies battled
at Actium in Greece, resulting in the defeat and eventual suicide
of both Anthony and his consort Cleopatra.

During the reign of Augustus, the Roman Empire was established; Augustus was the first emperor. He was an extremely

capable administrator, bringing many needed reforms to the empire. One of these was to divide the dominion of Rome into Senatorial and Imperial provinces. Senatorial provinces were generally peaceful, while Imperial provinces, which were in outlying regions, usually had rebellious subjects.

Judea became an Imperial province in A.D. 6. The Praefects firmly governed it, backed by a strong military garrison. Discontent with Rome was widespread, which lead to the rise of fervently anti-Roman groups like the Zealots. There were no major uprisings until the First Jewish Revolt, which began in A.D. 66.

The Emperor Tiberius.

In A.D. 14, the long reign of Augustus ended with his death, and the throne passed to Tiberius, the son of his consort Julia. Tiberius continued Augustus' efficient administration and was also a capable military commander. Like Augustus before him, he avoided war by not attempting to expand the borders of the empire.

During this time, the *Pax Romana* was maintained, bringing distinct benefits to the first Evangelists who spread the Gospel throughout the empire. Travel was secure on good roads, parts of which can still be seen today. At this time, Greek was the main language of the Roman world. The writing of the New Testament in Greek made it accessible to every corner of the empire.

An exception in this era of stability was the succession of Tiberius' demented grandnephew Gaius (Caligula) in A.D. 27. There was little mourning when his four-year reign ended. The empire was again in firm hands—the hands of Gaius' uncle, Claudius. Claudius continued the efficient administration of Augustus and Tiberius. It was largely during his rule that the ministry of the Apostle Paul took place.

Agrippina, Claudius' fourth wife, poisoned him in A.D. 54 so that her son Nero from a previous marriage could take the throne. Among the first casualties of Nero's rule were the early Christians. In A.D. 64, Rome was largely destroyed by fire, and the blaze that destroyed ten of 14 wards of the city was conveniently blamed on the Christians. The Apostles Paul and Peter are believed to have been martyred during this time.

With Nero's increasingly unpredictable behavior, Rome's golden age of stability ended. After his death by suicide in A.D. 68, confusion ruled as the throne passed hands three times in one year—in the midst of civil war. Vespasian, the first of the Flavian dynasty, was brought from suppressing the Jewish revolt in Judea to become emperor.

During the rule of Vespasian's son Domitian (A.D. 81–96), the situation of Christians deteriorated, and persecution was reported. Trajan, fourth in a line of Vespasian's successors, became Caesar in A.D. 98. The Christians had suffered sporadically before his rule, but Trajan began the first systematic persecution of the church. Some scholars believe that the persecution described in the Book of Revelation, written by the Apostle John at the end of the first century, reflects the rule of Trajan.

By this time, however, the church was no longer in its formative stage. The new faith of Christianity had become a commanding presence despite the fiendish opposition.

Ancient Mariners

ince the dawn of recorded history, men have taken to the seas. The earliest references to ships come from the Old Kingdom of Egypt, where as early as 2650 B.C., they brought cedar logs from Phoenicia on ships more than 170 feet in length. Egyptian reliefs also picture ships being used for military invasions and for ferrying captives.

A tomb painting from Thebes dated to the fifteenth century B.C. depicts sailing vessels with the same components familiar to mariners today, including masts with crow's nests, large rectangular sails, rudders, and oars.

Ships are also depicted in Assyrian reliefs as early as the eleventh century B.C., when Tiglath-pileser I sought to extend his power westward to the Mediterranean. From the time of Sennacherib, around 700 B.C., a three-decked warship is depicted with two levels of rowers and an upper deck where armed warriors sat.

Curiously, we have few pictures of the ships of the Phoenicians, who were renowned as masters of the sea. A large, sophisticated sailing vessel is beautifully depicted on a second-century B.C. sarcophagus. Its large square sail is unfurled from the mainmast, and a flag hangs from the high curled stern.

At the time of the New Testament, the Roman Empire was in command of the seas. A relief now in the Vatican depicts a warship propelled by 36 oars on two levels. The ship had an estimated crew of more than 200, with an outside gangway, main deck, and raised platforms for three levels of fighting men. With an estimated length of 103 feet and a displacement of 81 tons, the ship was of moderate size for its time.

Until the development of scuba-diving equipment, our knowledge of ancient ships was limited to references in contemporary literature and pictorial representations. Underwater archaeology has found the remains of hundreds of ancient sailing vessels built between the seventh century B.C. and the seventh century A.D.

Cargo is invariably found at the sites of underwater wrecks. Grain, oil, and wine were common foodstuffs transported by sea. The remains of dried fish, nuts, olives, and pitch have also been found. Unlike the hull of the ship, which eventually disintegrates, the barrels and clay jars (amphoras) used as containers for foods and liquids have survived through the centuries.

Several ships uncovered were more than a hundred feet long. The largest was about one hundred forty feet, with a length-to-beam ratio between three to one and four to one.

Shipwrights favored fir, cedar, or pine in the construction of hulls, but would use whatever wood was available. Since exposure to the elements decays wood, no intact ships have been found. However, a few hull bottoms, protected by the sea floor and overlaying cargo, have survived. They tell us much about how Greek and Roman ships were constructed.

Unlike the modern technique of shipbuilding, which begins with a skeleton to which an outer wooden or metal skin is fastened, the ancients used the opposite method. A shell of planks was first crafted, joined by close-set mortars and interlocking joints. Into this sturdy shell they then inserted and attached a set of frames with wooden dowels, making for an immensely strong hull.

This type of construction was necessary for the often treacherous waters of the Mediterranean, a sea that is practically littered with ships that failed to reach their destination.

No Miracle for the Miracle Worker?

 o one was better qualified than the Apostle Paul to be an expert on miracles and healing. Not only did he heal others, but he had experienced miraculous healing in his own life.

The Book of Acts relates how Paul was stoned and left for dead: "They stoned Paul and dragged him outside the city, thinking he was dead. But after the disciples had gathered around him, he got up and went back into the city" (Acts 14:20).

It is not clear here whether Paul had actually died. Nevertheless, he still experienced a miraculous healing. Stoning was a serious business and was usually fatal. Loss of consciousness constitutes severe injury.

On another occasion, a young man fell asleep while Paul was preaching. He fell from the third story and was taken up dead: "Paul went down, threw himself on the young man and put his arms around him. 'Don't be alarmed,' he said, 'He's alive!' Then he went upstairs again and broke bread and ate. After talking until daylight, he left. The people took the young man home alive and were greatly comforted" (Acts 20:10–12).

After the shipwreck on Malta, Paul had another miraculous healing. It happened as he gathered wood on the beach: " . . . as he put it on the fire, a viper, driven out by the heat, fastened itself on his hand. . . . But Paul shook the snake off into the fire and suffered no ill effects. The people expected him to swell up or suddenly fall over dead, but after waiting for a long time and seeing nothing unusual happen to him, they changed their minds and said he was a god" (Acts 28:3–6).

Paul stands and talks with Peter.

Verse 9 adds that Paul healed the father of the chief official of Malta, along with many others: "When this had happened, the rest of the sick on the island came and were cured."

Paul taught the churches in his care to practice healing. In his letter to the church in Corinth, he includes the "gift of healing" in his list of spiritual gifts.

Thus it is all the more puzzling to learn that both Paul and his associates suffered maladies that were not healed. His trusted helper Timothy had recurring stomach problems, for which Paul offered some practical advice: "Stop drinking only water, and use a little wine because of your stomach and your frequent illnesses" (1 Timothy 5:23).

A bit of advice about drinking wine seems a pale substitute for physical healing. Why didn't Paul just heal his friend?

Paul's inability on occasion to heal the illnesses of others was matched by his own chronic malady, which he called his "thorn in the flesh": "To keep me from becoming conceited because of these surpassing great revelations, there was given me a thorn in my flesh, a messenger of Satan, to torment me. Three times I pleaded with the Lord to take it away from me. But he said to me, 'My grace is sufficient for you, for my power is made perfect in weakness'" (2 Corinthians 12:7–9).

After experiencing such dramatic miracles, how could Paul fail to see healing in his own life? There are no easy answers, and Paul's "thorn in the flesh" has become a thorny issue for many theologians. Some try to avoid the issue of why Paul was not healed by suggesting that his "thorn" was a spiritual temptation, not a physical problem.

But we read in Galatians that Paul was indeed troubled by a physical illness: "As you know, it was because of an illness that I first preached the Gospel to you. Even though my illness was a trial to you, you did not treat me with contempt or scorn" (Galatians 4:13–14).

Scholars have suggested various ideas as to what Paul's ailment was. One prominent theory is that he suffered from a disease of the eyes. We have an indication of this in the same passage where he mentions his "illness," when he says: "For I tesify that, had it been possible, you would have torn out your eyes and given them to me" (Galatians 4:15).

At the end of his letter to the Galatians, he makes the following comment: "See what large letters I use as I write to you with my own hand!" (Galatians 6:11). This is another indication that his sight was not good. Some

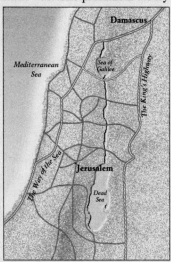

Paul journeyed from Jerusalem to Damascus in order to persecute Christians there.

have speculated that his eye problems originated when he was temporarily blinded during his conversion experience on the road to Damascus.

We may never know with any certainty what Paul's ailment was. But he was able to accept his trouble because he believed it was "to keep me from becoming conceited because of these surpassing great revelations."

Paul's Radical View of Marriage

 heologians and scholars have long suspected the Apostle Paul of harboring a negative opinion of women. They also believe he had a repressive view of the institution of marriage. But compared to the social mores of the culture in which he lived and ministered, Paul's teachings can be seen as nothing short of revolutionary.

Up until the time of the emperor Augustine, Roman society had a utilitarian view of marriage, the purpose of which was to produce heirs to inherit one's property and continue the family name. A husband was fully justified in divorcing his wife solely on the grounds that she was unable to bear children.

In the Roman concept of the *paterfamilias,* the husband virtually ruled over his wife, who was little more than a housekeeper. The purpose of marital relations was not mutual sexual pleasure but for the purpose of procreation. It was common for Roman men to look beyond home and hearth to prostitutes for their sexual satisfaction.

In fact, increasing numbers of men were finding their pleasures elsewhere and not bothering to marry. Augustus, concerned that the institution of marriage upon which society was built was endangered, decided to redress the growing reluctance to marry. Accordingly, in 18 B.C. he proclaimed new laws that imposed heavier taxes upon unmarried men and women, while granting financial benefits for those who married and had children.

After Augustus' new regulations went into force, more Roman men chose to marry, but without the intention of entering into a monogamous relationship. Prostitution continued to flourish, just as it had before.

It is this practice that Paul is referring to when writing to the Church in the Roman city of Corinth: "But because of cases of sexual immorality, each man should have his own wife and each woman her own husband. The husband should give to his wife her conjugal rights, and likewise the wife her husband. For the wife does not have authority over her own body, but the husband does; likewise the husband does not have authority over his own body, but the wife does" (1 Corinthians 7:2–4).

Paul's teaching here is a radical departure from established Roman custom regarding the relationship between husbands and wives. It granted hitherto unknown rights to wives and placed them on an equal basis with their husbands. His statement that a wife has authority over her husband's body in particular must have been greeted with shock by the typical Roman husband who until then had considered himself free to seek sexual pleasure outside of marriage.

The teaching of the New Testament regarding marriage eventually won the day and set a standard for Western civilization that has lasted for more than 19 centuries. While often taken for granted and increasingly challenged, the ideal of a mutual, monogamous relationship in which two people commit themselves exclusively to each other is still reflected in the marriage vows of lands that have come under the influence of the teaching of the Apostle Paul.

Towns of the Epistles
New Testament Cities:
What Happened at Philippi?

n his second missionary journey, the Apostle Paul visited the city of Philippi, "a leading city of the district of Macedonia and a Roman colony" (Acts 16:12). We know from the New Testament letter to the Philippians that he established a church there.

Located in the Roman province of Macedonia, Philippi was approximately ten miles inland from the Aegean Sea. It was situated on the Via Egnatia, the main overland route from Asia to the West. The city was greatly enlarged and developed by Philip II of Macedonia (359–336 B.C.), whose name it takes. Philippi gained fame as the site of a decisive battle in 42 B.C. in which Anthony and Octavian defeated Brutus and Cassius.

Archaeological excavations conducted at Philippi between 1914 and 1938 may have uncovered the site where Paul ministered at Philippi: "On the Sabbath day we went outside the gate by the river, where we supposed there was a place of prayer; and we sat down and spoke to the women who had gathered there" (Acts 16:13).

One mile from the city are the remains of a Roman ceremonial arch near the Gangites River. The arch was likely erected when Philippi became a Roman colony. The arch could also mark the *pomerium* or outer limits of the city. Inside the *pomerium* line, certain activities were restricted. Some, like buri-

Who Invented the Synagogue?

Many scholars believe the roots of the synagogue can be traced to the period after the Temple was destroyed and the Jewish people found themselves in exile. Since the Jews could no longer go to Jerusalem to worship, it became necessary to develop another means of worshiping. The synagogue was a place for the reading of the law, prayer, and teaching, unlike a Temple.

When the Jews returned to Jerusalem, they continued the institution of the synagogue, even after the Temple was rebuilt. Josephus mentions several synagogues in Galilee.

As an adult, Jesus attended the synagogue in Nazareth. According to the Gospels, Jesus frequently met with opposition while preaching in synagogues.

The earliest excavated remains of a synagogue are at the Dead Sea mountain fortress of Masada. Dated to the rule of Herod the Great (37–4 B.C.), the synagogue probably served the Jewish members of Herod's family, servants, and guests who desired a place for Sabbath worship there.

Fragments of biblical manuscripts were found buried under the floor of the synagogue at Masada. The placing of old manuscripts in hidden niches was a familiar practice for the Jewish people, since it was considered a desecration to burn or otherwise destroy copies of the Torah or other biblical books.

In 1890, workers discovered a hidden room in the ancient synagogue in Cairo. This *genizah*—literally "hiding place"—held a treasure trove of biblical scrolls only to be outdone a half-century later by the discovery of the Dead Sea Scrolls.

By the first century A.D., synagogues had spread from Judea to many other places. The Egyptian-Jewish writer and philosopher Philo attests to the existence of numerous synagogues in Alexandria, and Paul found Jewish synagogues as he traveled throughout the Roman empire.

In the early days of the church, some Jews who converted to Christianity remained in their synagogue. However, as time passed they were forced out of the synagogues and began meeting in homes.

al, were prohibited for obvious sanitary reasons. The *pomerium* was also used to restrict activities within the city that were deemed unsuitable, such as those associated with foreign religious cults.

Unlike other cities in which Paul evangelized, we find no mention of a synagogue in Philippi. At various times and places in the Roman Empire, Judaism was considered a foreign cult, and it is likely that this was the case at Philippi when Paul arrived. This explains why he found the women meeting down at the river, outside the *pomerium*.

It was at the river that Paul found his first convert: "A certain woman named Lydia, a worshiper of God, was listening to us; she was from the city of Thyatira and a dealer in purple cloth. The Lord opened her heart to listen eagerly to what was said by Paul" (Acts 16:14).

Archaeologists found ample evidence of a Christian community founded by Paul that thrived for centuries at Philippi.

New Testament Cities: Is Peter Buried in Rome?

 o city in the ancient world compared in size or grandeur to Rome. Pliny the Elder, governor of the province of Bithynia, writes that in A.D. 73 the walls of Rome measured more than 13 miles in circumference. The city was divided into 14 districts and had 265 street intersections.

Some of the magnificent public buildings of Rome, including the Colosseum, the Pantheon, and numerous temples, can still be seen today. Others, including the Circus Maximus, which held 150,000 people, and the theater of Pompey, which held 40,000, are only known from ancient sources.

While the rich lived in villas on the hills of the city, the poor lived in crowded districts in multistory tenements subject to collapse or fire. Rome had an extensive public welfare system that distributed wheat to most citizens at no cost. Water was also free and abundant, provided by several aqueducts to the city.

The emperor Augustine established police and fire-fighting forces in the city. Arson was considered a particularly evil crime and carried severe penalties. The concern was justified by the fire

System of the Roman aqueduct.

of A.D. 64, which destroyed an estimated ten of Rome's 14 districts.

Like many modern cities, Rome had become such a melting pot of nationalities that its citizens complained Rome was no longer Roman. The foreigners brought their own traditions and religions and found mutual support in their own culturally isolated groups. The Jews would have constituted one of these tolerated underclasses of Rome. Like other foreign groups, they were allowed to build their places of worship. The names of at least 13 synagogues in Rome are known from ancient sources.

An ancient cemetery has been excavated under St. Peter's Basilica in the Vatican. Both St. Peter's Basilica and the original fourth-century church that occupied the site were built in an area that contained pagan mausoleums and other structures dated to the second century. Christians were buried in pagan cemeteries until the third century. Although no bones have been uncovered that might be those of the apostle, the early and continuous reverence toward the site indicates that Peter may indeed have been buried here.

Other early material evidence of the Christians of Rome is found in the catacombs, extensive underground burial areas where believers buried their dead and gathered during time of persecution.

Excavations under churches in the city have also revealed homes of the late second and early third centuries that had been transformed into places of worship. These homes were generally located in the poor and populous districts of the city. However, there were also converts to the new faith of Christianity in

To an Unknown God

Paul's second missionary journey took him to Athens, in Greece, the cultural center of the ancient world. There, distressed to see that the city was full of idols, he spent his days evangelizing in the synagogue, the marketplace, or wherever people would listen.

After he debated some Epicureans and Stoics, they were sufficiently impressed to invite him to the Areopagus, located on a height overlooking the city. The Areopagus was where philosophers gathered for debate and discussion: "Now all the Athenians and the foreigners living there would spend their time in nothing but telling or hearing something new" (Acts 17:21).

Paul stood up before those gathered at the Areopagus and judiciously began his speech with a point of reference from something he had observed in the city: "Athenians, I see how extremely religious you are in every way. For as I went through the city and looked carefully at the objects of your worship, I found among them an altar with the inscription, 'To an unknown god.' What therefore you worship as unknown, this I proclaim to you" (Acts 17:22–23). He then went on to use the theme of the unknown God to introduce the monotheistic theme of the one true God who is the creator and lord of the universe.

Even though no inscription with precisely this wording in the singular has yet been discovered, it is known from ancient literature that the Greeks were careful to affirm the existence of unknown gods. This was because, being polytheists, they believed in many gods and wanted to ensure they would not fail to acknowledge any.

Ancient sources mention the existence of various altars dedicated to "unknown gods" on the road from Phalerum to Athens and also at Olympia. The Greek writer Diogenes Laertius tells of how, during a plague, the Athenians were advised to sacrifice to "the appropriate god"—in other words, the unknown god responsible for the plague.

The essence of Paul's message to the Athenians is that given by Jesus himself in speaking to the Samaritan woman: "You worship what you do not know; we worship what we know, for salvation is from the Jews" (John 4:22).

influential quarters. In his letter to the Philippians, the Apostle Paul writes: "All the saints greet you, especially those of the emperor's household" (Philippians 4:22).

New Testament Cities: Was Paul at the Games in Corinth?

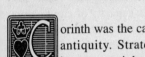orinth was the capital of Achaia and a major city of antiquity. Strategically situated on the isthmus between mainland Greece and the Peloponnesus, it controlled commerce between ports on the Gulf of Corinth and the Saronic Gulf.

Sections of a specially constructed roadway between the two ports, used for transporting boats over land on rollers, can still be seen today. This three-mile route saved ships from an often hazardous 200-mile voyage around the southern end of the Greek peninsula. In 1893, a canal across the isthmus was completed, connecting the Aegean Sea with the Adriatic.

Excavations at Corinth shed light on Paul's well-known letters to the church there, and to the Romans, which were written while he was at Corinth. In Chapter 16 of Romans, Paul sends greetings to the Roman church: "Gaius, who is host to me and to the whole church, greets you. Erastus, the city treasurer, and our brother Quartus, greet you" (Romans 16:23).

In 1929, a pavement inscription was uncovered that was dated to the latter half of the first century. The original bronze letters were torn out by looters, but the text could still be read: "Erastus in return for his aedileship laid [the pavement] at his own expense." In ancient Rome, an "aedile" was similar to a commissioner of public works.

The name Erastus is not common, and there is no other official known to have this name. Thus it seems fairly certain that this is the very official mentioned by Paul who was evidently also a member of the Christian congregation at Ephesus. It is likely that Erastus first served in the lower capacity of city treasurer before being promoted to aedile.

Paul's custom on his missionary journeys was to seek out the Jewish community of a city, which he did on his first visit: "When they reached Ephesus, he left them there, but first he himself went into the synagogue and had a discussion with the Jews" (Acts 18:19). That brief visit bore fruit, for when he returned to spend 18 months there in about A.D. 50, a small group of believers had already formed.

A piece of a marble doorway of uncertain date has been found that evidently was part of the Jewish synagogue of Corinth. The restored inscription, written in Greek, reads: "Synagogue of the Hebrews." Another fragment of marble is decorated with Jewish ritual objects: a menorah, palm branches, and citron.

Since the sixth century B.C., Corinth sponsored the biennial Isthmian Games, a Panhellenic festival of athletic contests dedicated to the sea god Poseidon. Paul would have witnessed the opening of the A.D. 51 festival, and in his letter to the Corinthians, his observations are applied to spiritual self-discipline: "Do you not know that in a race the runners all compete, but only one receives the prize? Run in such a way that you may win it. Athletes exercise self-control in all things; they do it to receive a perishable wreath, but we an imperishable one. So I do not run aimlessly, nor do I box as though beating the air; but I punish my body and enslave it, so that after proclaiming to others I myself should not be disqualified" (1 Corinthians 9:24–27).

It was a message that the Corinthian church, known for its moral and spiritual laxity, sorely needed to hear, and which Paul apparently exemplified in his own life.

New Testament Cities: The "Beasts" of Ephesus

phesus, located on a gulf of the Aegean Sea, was a political and commercial center of Asia Minor. A magnificent avenue, 35 feet wide and lined with columns, led from the harbor to the center of the city.

When the Apostle Paul visited and established a church there in the mid-first century, Ephesus was at the peak of its grandeur. With an estimated population of 250,000 it is believed to have been the fourth largest city in the world. Later, during the reign of the emperor Hadrian in the early second century, the city became the capital of the Roman province of Asia.

Since ancient times, the inhabitants of Ephesus worshiped Artemis, the Greek goddess of fertility. The Temple of Artemis

The Temple of Artemis in Ephesus.

at Ephesus, considered one of the seven wonders of the ancient world, appears on Roman coins of the day.

Artisans in the city prospered through the production of small figurines of the goddess Artemis. When Paul visited Ephesus during his second missionary journey, his preaching about the one true God stirred up the polytheistic vendors. One of them, a silversmith named Demetrius, instigated a riot when he called together his fellow silver workers.

His speech is recorded in the Book of Ephesians: "'Men, you know that we get our wealth from this business. You also see and hear that not only in Ephesus, but in almost the whole of Asia, this Paul has persuaded and drawn away a considerable number of people by saying that gods made with hands are not gods. And there is danger not only that this trade of ours may come into disrepute, but also that the temple of the great goddess Artemis will be scorned, and she will be deprived of her majesty, which brought all of Asia and the world to worship her.' When they heard this, they were enraged and shouted, 'Great is Artemis of the Ephesians!'" (Acts 19:25–28).

The city was stirred up, and a mob made for the theater, dragging two of Paul's companions with them. The theater of Ephesus has been excavated and is visible today as an imposing tiered edifice that seated 24,000 people. The text aptly describes the chaos that reigned: "Meanwhile, some were shouting one thing, some another; for the assembly was in confusion, and most of them did not know why they had come together" (Acts 19:32).

Fortunately, the magistrate of the city persuaded the crowd not to harm the evangelists, who were able to leave the city without further incident. In writing to the church at Corinth, Paul mentions that he "fought with wild animals at Ephesus" (1 Corinthians 15:32). It is not known whether he meant literal or figurative wild animals.

Ephesus also served as a center for the imperial cult of Rome, which was centered around the worship of the reigning emperor and preceding emperors.

According to Christian tradition, the Apostle John moved to Ephesus and died there at an advanced age. At the time John is thought to have resided there, the city had a temple and cult dedicated to the ruling Flavian dynasty, and John likely wrote during the rule of Domitian (A.D. 81–96). Some scholars believe that much of John's use of imagery in the Book of Revelation, such as worship of the "Beast," refers to the imperial cult prevalent at Ephesus.

Much of prophecy is thought to have a dual reference, in that the prophet uses the language, culture, and circumstances of his day to describe events destined to occur far in the future. If so, the "Beast" of Revelation, who demands worship and instigates a worldwide conflagration, may not be only a fearful personage from the past, but may also be a symbol of Satan, whose work, according to Scriptures, is far from completed.

ST. JOHN'S REVELATION
The Seven Cities

he Book of Revelation is filled with illustrative detail; for most modern readers, it is difficult to understand. This apocalyptic—or prophetic—writing was directed to the early Christians in Asia Minor.

The letters to seven churches in chapters two and three of the Book of Revelation have long been a source of scholarly controversy. One view is that they represent seven types of churches present in all ages. That is, the strengths and weaknesses mentioned regarding each of the seven churches can be found in the Christian Church in all ages.

Another view is that the seven churches represent a historical progression, and that each church symbolizes the state of the Church in a different age. The difficulty with this view is that few students of the Bible have agreed about which churches represent which times.

A third view is that the seven churches of Revelation refer primarily to churches in the first century. But the admonitions given to each can apply to churches and Christians of all eras.

The churches are congregations in seven cities of first-century Asia Minor: Ephesus, Smyrna, Pergamum, Thyatira, Sardis, Philadelphia, and Laodicea. It isn't known why these particular churches were chosen. However, the order in which John lists the cities in Revelation corresponds to their actual location on a circuitous route in Asia Minor, the likely route used by government messengers and itinerant Christian evangelists and teachers.

Particular characteristics of each city are found in each letter. John commends the Ephesians, for example, for their love of the truth, but they are urged to remember their earlier love, which evidently had begun to wane. Some commentators suggest the Ephesians had fallen into a comfortable accommodation with the pagan imperial cult prevalent in the city.

Smyrna was a large and prosperous coastal city 40 miles north of Ephesus. John warns the church there about hostile Jews who are called the "synagogue of Satan." They persecuted Christians in the city with the complicity of the Jewish population. The most famous example was Polycarp, one of the first

The Seven Cities of Revelation.

martyrs of the church, who was put to death in Smyrna at the instigation of the Jews of the city.

Some 50 miles northeast of Smyrna lies the ruins of Pergamum, an impressive capital city in the first century. Pergamum is described as the location of "Satan's throne," a possible reference to the fact that the city was the official center for the imperial cult in Asia. One of the most imposing pagan edifices was the great altar of Zeus, high on the mountain above.

The overland route continues to Thyatira, a center for manufacturing and marketing. The church there was warned against learning the "deep things of Satan," a possible reference to the pagan guild feasts, which the rest of the city would have participated in. Apparently, a woman known as Jezebel was stirring up trouble in the church at Thyatira and is condemned in the strongest terms.

Sardis, located 45 miles east of Thyatira, had an illustrious history as the ancient kingdom of Lydia. In 133 B.C., the city came under Roman control and was known for its wealth. The church at Sardis was severely criticized and warned to be watchful: "Remember then what you received and heard; obey it, and repent. If you do not wake up, I will come like a thief, and you will not know at what hour I will come to you" (Revelation 3:3). This was a message the people of Sardis needed to hear, for twice in its history the city was conquered when its defenders were caught off guard.

Thirty miles beyond Sardis lies Philadelphia, the sixth city along the route. Philadelphia was a prosperous agricultural and industrial center. Its main drawback was that it was prone to devastating earthquakes. The Philadelphians are promised an unshakable city: If they remain faithful, they are told, they will become like an unmovable pillar in the new Jerusalem.

The last city, Laodicea, was the wealthiest city in Phrygia during Roman times. The Laodiceans were criticized for their spiritual poverty: "Therefore I counsel you to buy from me gold refined by fire so that you may be rich; and white robes to clothe you and to keep the shame of your nakedness from being seen;

and salve to anoint your eyes so that you may see" (Revelation 3:18).

Laodicea was famous for its medical school. One of the medicines produced in the city was an eye-salve made from a substance called "Phrygian powder" and olive oil. It became a fitting illustration of the Laodicean's spiritual blindness.

The Laodiceans were also criticized for their lukewarm faith. They were "neither hot nor cold" (Revelation 3:15–16). Interestingly, Laodicea was located seven miles south of Hierapolis, a source of famous hot-water springs. It was less than 10 miles from Colossae, a source of cool water. Laodicea was in between—both spiritually and geographically.

A Nefarious World Leader

The Book of Revelation tells us that at the end of the age a mysterious figure of consummate evil will arise: "The beast was given a mouth uttering haughty and blasphemous words, and it was allowed to exercise authority for 42 months. It opened its mouth to utter blasphemies against God, blaspheming his name and his dwelling, that is, those who dwell in heaven. Also it was allowed to make war on the saints and to conquer them. It was given authority over every tribe and people and language and nation" (Revelation 13:5–7).

World history is the story of great empires. None of them, however, could dominate the world's political system to the degree portrayed here.

Satan, bound in chains.

We read that the Beast of Revelation will also exercise complete authority over the economic affairs of the world: "Also it causes all, both small and great, both rich and poor, both free and slave, to be marked on the right hand or the forehead, so that no one can buy or sell who does not have the mark, that is, the name of the beast or the number of its name" (Revelation 13:16–17).

The Antichrist, or beast, along with the false prophet mentioned in Revelation 16, will make war with the saints and lead the world in a final rebellion against God. Their leader is Satan, the "great red dragon" mentioned in the twelfth chapter of Revelation.

All the peoples of the world will be commanded to bow before the Antichrist: "And all the inhabitants of the earth will worship it, everyone whose name has not been written from the foundation of the world in the book of life of the Lamb that was slaughtered" (Revelation 13:8).

The Antichrist will be able to perform unimaginable feats: "And it was allowed to give breath to the image of the beast so that the image of the beast could even speak and cause those who would not worship the image of the beast to be killed" (Revelation 13:15).

Some biblical scholars believe that the Antichrist is a symbolic reference to the forces of evil. Others conclude that the passages speak of a political ruler who will rise one day and exercise his power over the nations of the world.

The Lawless One

Christians have traditionally referred to the man of consummate evil who will arise at the end of days to deceive the nations as the Antichrist. However, nowhere in the Bible is the word used to refer to a person. It appears only in the Book of 1 John in an impersonal sense: "And every spirit that does not confess Jesus is not from God. And this is the spirit of the antichrist, of which you have heard that it is coming; and now it is already in the world" (1 John 4:3).

Other passages speak of a personal manifestation of evil yet to come in the future. These would include the "beast" in the Book of Revelation and the "prince" and "willful king" of the Book of Daniel. In addition to these cryptic passages, the Apostle Paul gives a fuller description of this mysterious person whom he calls "the lawless one":

"He opposes and exalts himself above every so-called god or object of worship, so that he takes his seat in the temple of God, declaring himself to be God... And then the lawless one will be revealed, whom the Lord Jesus will destroy with the breath of his mouth, annihilating him by the manifestation of his coming. The coming of the lawless one is apparent in the working of Satan, who uses all power, signs, lying wonders, and every kind of wicked deception for those who are perishing, because they refused to love the truth and so be saved. For this reason God sends them a powerful delusion, leading them to believe what is false, so that all who have not believed the truth but took pleasure in unrighteousness will be condemned" (2 Thessalonians 2:4, 8–12).

The Mark of the Beast

opular books on the subject of biblical prophecies have abounded with theories as to the identification of the Antichrist. Some wild attempts have been made to connect this individual to a cryptic verse in Revelation: "This calls for wisdom: let anyone with understanding calculate the number of the beast, for it is the number of a person. Its number is six hundred sixty-six" (Revelation 13:18).

The numerical value of more than one prominent political figure's name has been equated to that number. Others suggest that 666 refers to the Social Security number of the Antichrist, or perhaps some computerized identification code of the future.

Few of these various attempts to interpret the meaning of 666 take into account the historical context of the verse in Revelation that speaks about the number. The modern mind may consider it strange to designate someone's name by a number, but those living at the end of the first century, when Revelation was written, would have understood the writer's intention.

The Apostle John was in all likelihood employing Gematria, the practice of discovering hidden meaning in a word by computing its numerical value. This method of interpreting words and texts was common in the ancient world of the Hebrews and Greeks, as both Hebrew and Greek used the letters of the alphabet to denote numbers, lending themselves to Gematria.

Some early Christian documents, for example, use 888 for the name of Jesus in Greek. Graffiti on excavated walls of Pompeii provides further examples of the common practice of assigning numerical values to names. Rabbis also sought hidden meanings in the Hebrew Scriptures through Gematria.

Accordingly, the attempts of the early Church to decipher the meaning of the 3 sixes focused on the numerical value of the names of possible Antichrist candidates. Church father Irenaeus of Lyons, for example, records several possibilities in the Greek language, but seems not to have considered any in Hebrew.

The Book of Revelation, however, was written by the Apostle John, a Jew from Galilee. Although the text of Revelation was written in Greek, the language of the Roman world, John would have been more familiar with Hebrew Gematria than its Greek counterpart.

So it is not surprising to discover that the Hebrew translation of the Greek for *Caesar Nero* adds up to the required 666. This does not necessarily mean that the Apostle John believed Nero was the Antichrist. He may have been pointing his readers to Nero as a forerunner of the coming Antichrist, exhibiting characteristics of the future Beast of Revelation.

Antichrist Candidates: The Minstrel Emperor

 y the year A.D. 68, Rome was in turmoil. The enemies of Lucius Domitius Nero, the reigning Caesar for the preceding 14 years, were finally gaining the upper hand. The man whose reign had begun with such promise had degenerated into a wandering minstrel obsessed with grandiose illusions. He was no longer fit to rule.

In his very first speech to the Senate, Nero promised a new Golden Age, and for the first five years of his reign he exhibited generosity and moderation toward his subjects. Historians record a long list of noteworthy improvements in the political and social life of Rome, including an end to capital punishment and the blood circuses.

But by A.D. 59, Nero had snapped. He embarked upon a reign of terror that most probably resulted in the deaths (among countless others) of the Apostles Peter and Paul in Rome. That same year he consented to the assassination of Agrippina, his increasingly insane mother who had ruthlessly engineered his rise to power.

The notorious fire that ravaged Rome for nine days in A.D. 64, consumed much of the city. Nero was blamed, although at the time of the fire he was at his villa in Antium, 35 miles away. A newly established religious sect—Christianity—was also blamed for starting the fire, an accusation that Nero encouraged.

The following year, Nero put down a revolt with brutal force, resulting in the deaths of Seneca and the poet Lucan, as well as many others innocent of the conspiracy.

A lesser-known side of Nero began to appear, that of an aspiring poet, lyre player, and theatrical performer. He was also deeply attracted to mystical religions. He dabbled in Zoroastrianism, Gnosticism, and perhaps even Christianity (as indicated by a fresco in the Palantine Chapel depicting Nero and the Apostle Paul having a conversation).

At the end of A.D. 66, smitten by the Siren's call from the land of the gods, Nero spent 15 months wandering throughout Greece as a barefoot ascetic, reciting poetry and playing his music. His obsession with mystical religions while the Empire was reeling from revolts in Africa, Gaul, and Spain, not to mention Judea, earned him the contempt of the Romans.

Nero, Emperor of Rome.

In blissful distraction, Nero occupied himself with composing songs and inventing a hydraulic organ on which to play his beloved music. He laughed at the growing threats to the Empire and at popular discontent at home, claiming, "I have only to appear and sing to have peace once again in Gaul!"

Condemned by the Senate to die a slave's death on the cross, abandoned even by his Praetorian Guard, Nero fled the city. Arriving at one of his villas outside Rome, and seeing that all hope was lost, Nero stabbed himself and was buried by his Christian mistress, Acte.

Well before Nero's death, the Christians in Rome were calling him the Antichrist for his attempts to deify himself by enforcing emperor worship. The fact that he died virtually alone, in an obscure place, passing from the scene without even a state funeral, led to rumors that the emperor was, in fact, not dead.

There was speculation that Nero had somehow managed to escape east to the Parthians, a dreaded enemy of Rome. From there, it was said, he would return to wreak a fearsome revenge on the city that had turned against him.

These rumors of revenge, though unfounded, spread rapidly throughout the Empire and continued even into the next century and beyond. Decrees appeared, allegedly from the hand of Nero, and Roman historians record no fewer than three instances in which impostors arose claiming to be the fallen emperor. One of these imposters actually managed to convince many Parthians that he was the emperor Nero, throwing Achaia and Asia Minor into terror.

These popular legends about Nero influenced the early Christians, and many considered him the Antichrist. As time passed, some thought he would rise from the dead to wage war against Rome. This battle would occur at the end of the world, prior to the second coming of Jesus Christ.

The apocalyptic *Ascension of Isaiah,* dated from the end of the first century, echoes this belief: "And after it has been brought to completion, Beliar will descend, the great angel, the king of this world, which he has ruled ever since it existed. He will descend from his firmament in the form of a man, a king of iniquity, a murderer of his mother—this is the king of this world." The description of the Antichrist as "a murderer of his mother" is, of course, a reference to Nero's assassination of his mother in A.D. 59.

Christian writers held the legend of Nero redivivus (Nero resurrected) long after the first century. Jerome, writing at the end of the fourth century, affirmed that it was still held by some Christians even in his day.

Antichrist Candidates: The Imperial Dictator

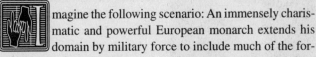 magine the following scenario: An immensely charismatic and powerful European monarch extends his domain by military force to include much of the former Roman Empire. His army marches on Rome itself, bringing the Pope into his sphere of influence with a peace treaty.

Next comes the Middle East. He occupies Egypt by force and invades the Holy Land. Marching up the coastline at the head of a powerful army, he invades the land of Israel. His army camps at the very mouth of the plain of Megiddo, the traditional location of the prophetic battle of Armageddon. He journeys to the ancient site of Megiddo overlooking the expansive valley. Looking down from the summit, he observes that the setting is an ideal site for a battle of epic proportions.

To many students of biblical prophecies, this description reads like a page out of the Book of Daniel or the Book of Revelation. But this scenario is not destined to occur in the future; it played itself out 200 years ago during the reign of Napoleon Bonaparte.

The parallels between the greatest imperial dictator of European history and the biblical description of the Antichrist are amazing. For starters, Napoleon was very nearly an Italian subject, recalling the biblical passages linking the Antichrist with the revived Roman Empire. His mother tongue was a dialect of

Italian. His place of origin, Corsica, was an island off the Italian mainland, the language and culture of which are closely allied with Italy. Fifteen months prior to Napoleon's birth, Corsica was deeded to France.

After a military education and commission as an artillery officer, Napoleon faltered in his career and was reduced to wandering the streets of Paris at half-pension and without a military assignment. As destiny would have it, a fresh opportunity presented itself when Napoleon was called upon for assistance during an uprising in Paris in 1795. He displayed strategic genius and decisiveness in suppressing the revolt, and he was rewarded by being appointed commander of the French occupation army of Italy.

Napoleon, as painted in his study.

The next few years brought dazzling success in a campaign against the Austrians fought on Italian soil. While the defeated Hapsburgs sued for peace, Napoleon turned his attention toward southern Italy. In an epic campaign, his army overcame all resistance on the Italian peninsula and occupied, significantly, the papal states.

Napoleon's conquest of the Vatican territories of the vicar of Rome excited the imagination of students of Bible prophecy. The banishment of the Pope was taken as fulfillment of the cryptic passage in Revelation 13, which speaks of the beast suffering a "mortal wound."

Even the numbers seemed to add up. The Beast of Revelation 13 "was given a mouth uttering haughty and blasphemous words, and it was allowed to exercise authority for 42 months" (Revelation 13:5). Forty-two months was taken (somewhat incorrectly) to mean 1,260 days, later taken to mean 1,260 years.

When 1,260 years are subtracted from the year of Napoleon's occupation of the papal states, one arrives at the magic number of 538, which happens to be the year of the beginning of papal power. Indeed, there is some justification for this, in that 538 happens to fall within the reign of Justinian, the greatest of the Byzantine Roman emperors.

Napoleon's next move reads like a page out of the Book of Daniel. He decided to invade Egypt to threaten the trade routes of England, his adversary. Accordingly, in 1798 he sailed with his army for Egypt, managing to elude the overwhelmingly superior fleet of Britain's Admiral Nelson. After defeating the Egyptian army in the shadow of the great pyramids, all opposition collapsed and his army of 38,000 troops easily won control of the country.

Trouble loomed when Turkey, within whose Ottoman Empire Egypt was forcibly enrolled, declared war upon France. Napoleon was forced to march up the coast into Palestine to secure the ports of Jaffa and Acre against the Turkish navy. This appeared to be a stunningly accurate fulfillment of a prophecy in the Book of Daniel: "At the time of the end . . . the king of the north shall rush upon him like a whirlwind, with chariots and horsemen, and with many ships" (Daniel 11:40).

Napoleon's army occupied Jaffa, but ground to a halt at Acre, which withstood his siege with help from the British fleet offshore. This appeared to fulfill yet another prophecy of Daniel: "For ships of Kittim shall come against him, and he shall lose heart and withdraw. He shall be enraged and take action against the holy covenant. He shall turn back and pay heed to those who forsake the holy covenant" (Daniel 11:30). "Kittim" is the tribal name for the island of Cyprus, and is used to refer to the lands beyond that island kingdom—perhaps, it was thought, as far away as Great Britain.

It seemed as if all the pieces of the puzzle were in place. However, instead of fighting the decisive battle of Armageddon, Napoleon withdrew from Palestine, confounding the hopes of those who hoped to witness the great final battle at the end of time.

Napoleon's fortunes eventually waned until he finally met his match in the Duke of Wellington at Waterloo in 1815. Shortly afterward, Napoleon was sent into exile. Another possible Antichrist had failed to live up to the grand expectations of prophecy enthusiasts.

Antichrist Candidates: Il Duce

In the midst of the two World Wars that dominated the first half of the twentieth century, a political and military leader emerged on the European continent who occupied the attention of prophecy teachers and their followers for more than a decade. Attention was focused on Adolf Hitler's fellow dictator to the south, Italy's Benito Mussolini.

Out of the tumult of the first World War rose the ex-schoolteacher who preached a fiery brand of nationalism and promised revival of an Italian empire, catching the attention of prophecy watchers, who believed that the Antichrist would arise out of a "revived Roman Empire." All eyes were on *Il Duce* ("the leader").

Mussolini was appointed premier in 1922. Two years later, following a rigged election won by terrorizing the opposition, his Fascists finally obtained a majority in the Italian cabinet. Mussolini promptly dissolved all rival political parties and inaugurated a one-party state.

Evidence was not long in coming that linked *Il Duce* with the Beast of Revelation. It seemed as though he fit the role of the egotistical, bombastic leader uttering "proud words and blasphemies" (Revelation 13:5), who was expected to rise out of Rome. Furthermore, with his signing of the Lateran Treaty and the Concordat of 1929, Mussolini was seen as joining forces with the Roman Catholic Church.

Mussolini's invasion of Ethiopia in October 1935 caused a commotion among those who study prophecy. On the one hand, it constituted a downward thrust into a region bordering the Middle East, which could be taken as a distraction preceding a thrust up into Israel for the Battle of Armageddon. They also noted that, in Ezekiel 38, Ethiopia is an ally of Gog, who leads an invasion of Israel.

In the end, however, it became clear that Mussolini did not possess the necessary military prowess of the Antichrist. His ineptness as a commander in one military campaign after another eventually disqualified him for consideration.

Long before Mussolini was unceremoniously shot by Italian partisans in 1945, the

Benito Mussolini, on the march.

"revived Roman Empire" of his pompous rhetoric had crumbled before the advancing Allied forces.

A Revived Roman Empire?

 popular belief among students of biblical prophecy is that, at the end of the world, the Roman Empire will rise from the ashes of history. With the Antichrist at its head, Rome will draw the armies of the world into the final battle of Armageddon.

Belief in a revived Roman Empire comes from a prophecy in the Book of Daniel: "After the sixty-two weeks, an anointed one shall be cut off and shall have nothing, and the troops of the prince who is to come shall destroy the city and the sanctuary. Its end shall come with a flood, and to the end there shall be war. Desolations are decreed" (Daniel 9:26).

In this passage, the "anointed one" is believed to refer to Jesus, who will be "cut off" or crucified. The text then states that Jerusalem will be destroyed by "the troops of the prince who is to come." From history we can infer that the troops mentioned here are the Roman legions that sacked the city in A.D. 70. Who, then, is "the prince who is to come"? This is understood by some to be a reference to the future Antichrist. For those who accept this, the Antichrist is here identified with Rome.

Additional clues are found in the chapter 13 of Revelation: "And I saw a beast rising out of the sea, having ten horns and seven heads; and on its horns were ten diadems, and on its heads were blasphemous names . . . And the dragon gave it his power and his throne and great authority. One of its heads seemed to have received a death-blow, but its mortal wound had been healed. In amazement the whole earth followed the beast" (Revelation 13:1–3).

As the chapter progresses, a political leader appears who exercises extraordinary supernatural powers, and who, according to many scholars, must be the Antichrist. The "ten horns and seven heads" may refer to political powers aligned with him.

We have already read how the Antichrist is connected with Rome in Daniel 9:26. If that identification is correct—and scholars are *not* of one mind on this issue—then it makes possible the identification of the "ten horns" as ten kings of a revived Roman Empire.

The efforts to unite Europe politically and economically in recent times caused a furor among some biblical prophecy enthusiasts. They eagerly awaited the tenth nation to join the European Economic Community (EEC), which they expected to be followed by the revealing of the Antichrist. However, those expectations failed to materialize as the EEC reached and then exceeded the symbolic number of ten member nations.

One explanation for why the prophetic passages of the Bible defy a common interpretation comes at the end of the Book of Daniel, when the prophet is told: "But you, Daniel, keep the words secret and the book sealed until the time of the end." (Daniel 12:4). This verse seems to say that the meaning of these mysterious passages is purposefully being withheld until some future time.

Who Are the 144,000?

 n Revelation, John witnesses a series of visions. The vision in Chapter Seven has intrigued students of the Bible through the centuries.

"I saw another angel ascending from the rising of the sun, having the seal of the living God, and he called with a loud voice to the four angels who had been given power to damage earth and sea, saying, 'Do not damage the earth or the sea or the trees, until we have marked the servants of our God with a seal on their foreheads.' And I heard the number of those who were sealed, one hundred forty-four thousand, sealed out of every tribe of the people of Israel" (Revelation 7:2–4).

Who are these 144,000 people, and when does their "sealing" take place? Some scholars take the number literally, based on the fact that this group is described in the text as coming from the 12 tribes of Israel. They are thought to be Jewish converts to Christianity who will evangelize the world.

Others point out that the original 12 tribes of Israel no longer exist as distinct entities. Ten were lost to history in the Assyrian captivity in 722 B.C. The remaining two tribes lost their separate identity after the fall of Jerusalem in A.D. 70.

Some take the figure to be symbolic. The squaring of the number twelve (12 tribes times 12 thousand) is taken as a way of emphasizing completeness. For these believers, 144,000 symbolizes the generation of faithful who will enter the final turbulent stage of human history when the forces of evil reach their peak. The "sealing" does not mean they will be spared persecution—indeed, the verse that follows describes a vision of a multitude of martyrs in Heaven. Rather, it symbolizes the promise of eternal life in Heaven when their life on earth is finished.

Assorted scholars believe the figure does not refer to all the faithful, but only to the number of martyrs in the last days of human history, during the final conflict with the forces of evil. However, a later passage describes a "great multitude that no one could count, from every nation, from all tribes and peoples and languages" who have come out of "the great ordeal" (Revelation

Doré's woodcut of St. John on the Island of Patmos.

7:9, 14). Thus it appears that the total number of martyrs exceeds 144,000 and is beyond counting.

Whether the number is to be taken literally or symbolically will remain a mystery until the last days.

The Last Battle

he Book of Revelation speaks about a final cosmic battle between the forces of good and evil. We read that the "kings of the whole world" will be assembled "for battle on the great day of God the Almighty.... And they assembled them at the place that in Hebrew is called Harmagedon" (Revelation 16:14, 16).

While other translations have the more familiar "Armaged-don" instead of "Harmagedon," many Christians through the centuries have interpreted Harmagedon to mean Mount Megiddo because the Hebrew word for mount is "har." Thus they place the future battle at the ancient site of the city of Megiddo.

Megiddo has been the site of several important battles in biblical history. It was in the Plain of Esdraelon that Deborah and Barak routed the Canaanite king, Sisera. In his zeal to destroy the house of Ahab, Jehu struck down Joram and ran King Ahaziah through with a spear—at Megiddo.

Later, Josiah would meet Pharaoh Neco II in battle at Megiddo, despite Neco's attempt to avert conflict: "But Neco sent envoys to him, saying, 'What have I to do with you, king of Judah? I am not coming against you today, but against the house with which I am at war; and God has commanded me to hurry. Cease opposing God, who is with me, so that he will not destroy you'" (2 Chronicles 35:21). Josiah would not be dissuaded and persisted at the cost of his own life.

The strategic value of Megiddo has been underscored through the ages. Napoleon Bonaparte, who fought a major battle against the Turks at nearby Acco, is said to have remarked that Megiddo would be an admirable location for a battle of cataclysmic proportions. In the twentieth century, British commander General Edmund Allenby drove the Turks from Palestine during World War I after capturing the pass.

Some scholars, however, reject the identification of Megiddo with the Armageddon mentioned in the Book of Revelation. There is no record of a mountain in either ancient or modern times called Mount Megiddo. An archaeological mound bears that name, but it hardly qualifies to be called a hill, much less a mountain.

Other descriptions of the future battle center around Jerusalem, in the central highlands, rather than on the Plain of Esdraelon. In the Book of Zechariah we read: "On that day I will make Jerusalem a heavy stone for all the peoples; all who lift it shall grievously hurt themselves. And all the nations of the earth shall come against it" (Zechariah 12:3).

Other suggested translations for "Armageddon" include "mount of assembly," "city of desire," and "his fruitful mountain," all of which could describe Jerusalem. A mediating position points out that the battle of Harmagedon is spoken of as taking place in the geographically limited land of Israel. Since the battle is described as involving massive armies, it is conceivable that it would not be confined to one battlefield. Thus, if the battle spreads from Jerusalem to the Valley of Esdraelon in the north, it would in effect encompass the views of both groups.

Epilogue

ecause we regard the Bible as the Word of God for one of the world's largest religious groups, it is innately mysterious. Even the early luminaries in the Bible were aware of the secrets and puzzles within the Kingdom of God. Daniel, a prophet of God, recorded: "No wise men, enchanters, magicians, or diviners can show to the king the mystery that the king is asking, but there is a God in heaven who reveals mysteries,..." (Daniel 2:27–28a). Another mystery! Does God provide clues to the secrets behind Scripture?

There can be no doubt that the Bible contains action, adventure, drama, love—the full range of human emotion—but what about mysteries? The biblical topics that people talk about or read about focus on the mysterious and unsolved. *Secrets of the Bible* unravels many of the inexplicable parts of Scripture, beginning with the Garden of Eden and ending with the revelation to St. John on the Isle of Patmos.

Through aerial photography, down-in-the-dirt archaeological digs, carbon-dating and other hi-tech equipment, new information is gathered every day. *Secrets of the Bible* includes that up-to-date information so as to cast light on secrets previously too complex or antiquated to solve.

To close this authoritative and thought-provoking book by writing "The End," would be inaccurate. There is no end to the secrets hidden within the Bible—nor to the solutions we can entertain as new and more-sophisticated equipment is developed. Perhaps it is better to end by saying... Amen.